I0707404

Marcus Deminco

ADHD – Attention Deficit Hyperactivity Disorder. Truth or Invention?

Translated by Ilka Andrade Suarez
Copyright © 2019 - Marcus Deminco
All Rights Reserved | Salvador – Bahia – Brazil
ISBN: 9781652416722
Independently Published

Formatting, layout and conversion for eBooks
Marlon Bellator
md.bellator@gmail.com
Cover Creation
Erick Cerqueira (Marketing & Design)
http://esc3d.com.br

D395s

Deminco, Marcus

ADHD – Attention Deficit Hyperactivity Disorder. Truth or Invention?/ Marcus Deminco – 1ª ed. – Salvador : Independently Published, 2019. Translated by Ilka Andrade Suarez
Marcus Deminco, 2019.
211 p.

ISBN: 9781652416722

1. Attention Deficit Hyperactivity Disorder. 2. Tests, Scales, Questionnaires, Diagnosis 3. Psychology. I. Title. Truth or Invention?, ADHD – Attention Deficit Hyperactivity Disorder.
I.,. II. Título.

CDD-658.45
CDU: 811.134.3

Scheda di catalogazione preparata dal sistema bibliotecario universitario (SIBI / UFBA)

ADHD
Attention Deficit Hyperactivity Disorder

Truth
or
Invention?

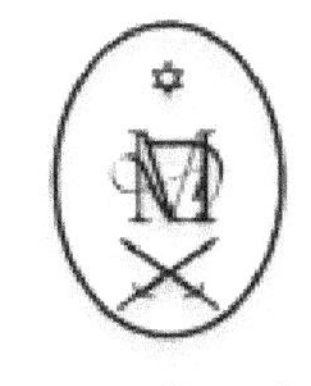

Marcus Deminco

Marcus Deminco

Translated by Ilka Andrade Suarez
Copyright © 2019 - Marcus Deminco
All Rights Reserved | Salvador – Bahia – Brazil
ISBN: 9781652416722
Independently Published

Marcus Deminco

Summary

Note About This Edition

Currently, Attention Deficit Hyperactivity Disorder (ADHD) is estimated to affect 2.5% of adults, about 3 to 7% of school-age children (6-12 years) worldwide, and in More than 68% of cases the disorder lasts for life.

Considering these numbers and the high prevalence of **ADHD**, the main purpose of this book is to make accessible a variety of instruments (Scales, Tests, Questionnaires, Diagnostic Criteria, Screening, etc.) that enable a better assessment of the existence of the diagnosis of Attention Deficit Hyperactivity Disorder (**ADHD**) in children, youth and adults. However, by no means do the resources available here - albeit of great value - have the character of asserting any diagnosis. It is noteworthy that the diagnosis of **ADHD** is strictly clinical, and no single tool replaces the thorough analysis performed by a specialized professional.

With regard to the constant news that casts doubt on the truth of the existence of **ADHD**, the book also soberly refutes these controversies, presenting compelling arguments. In addition, the book also features a list of celebrities diagnosed with **ADHD** and exciting testimonials from several people equally diagnosed with the disorder.

It is also important to highlight that - because much of the content of this book has been translated from other languages possibly some expressions and / or excerpts appear to be slightly inaccurate and / or ambiguous in language.

The Contradictory News About ADHD and Ritalin

Suddenly, several celebrities from all over the world diagnosed with Hyperactivity Attention Deficit Disorder (**ADHD**) have begun to make public details about their lives and experiences with the Disorder. Among the famous, Steve Jobs, Bill Gates, Steven Spielberg, Tom Cruise, Jim Carrey, Justin Timberlake, Will Smith, Danny Glover, Sylvester Stallone, Michael Jordan, Michael Phelps, Simone Biles, etc.

Consequently, **ADHD** began to symbolize a much less derogatory condition than those primitive ideas linked to limitations and/or disabilities. While possessing the Disorder, it even acquired a certain "status" of intelligence, of prodigiousness. As being a more frequent condition among differentiated, talented, creative people, extraordinary athletes, etc.

However, if the then watch that had never measured my time in accordance with the ordinary chronology of other men was finally synchronized; if just at that moment, perhaps for the first time in my entire life, I was in the perfect agreement with the events of the contemporary world, I had little time to enjoy that unpretentious punctuality of mine. For almost simultaneously, there were also beginning to emerge numerous matters trying to unframe me, leaving me out of the only situation in which I had not delayed myself. As if they wanted to put me back in the post of retarder, several factoids began to disclose that that disorder I had, already diagnosed eleven years ago, but now in full fashion, on the most favorable occasion, would simply not exist.

However, among the most varied fabulated news, some deserve — even in mutual lack of worthiness — a certain highlight. During the first half of 2013, for example, a headline replicated by several media outlets questioned and answered at the same time: "Why did French children lack attention deficit? " In their descriptive content, the reports claimed — with the property of those who could at most assume that — educational philosophy, along with a holistic psychosocial approach by French mental health experts —made hyperactivity Care Deficit Disorder **(ADHD)** simply disappear, or be able to reduce its incidence in tiny numbers.

But how to ignore one's own ignorance is the main feature of the ignorant, driven by an irrational urge to slight bare all his stupidity, these journalists, columnists, bloggers and so many other functional illiterate, self-educated by the presumption of what they think they know -- without even knowing for sure what they think -- they didn't even bother to investigate the origin of these sources, or to find out —even if it was through a quick google search —the veracity of the blunders before they reproduce. But, as Aristotle says, "The ignorant says, the wise man doubts, and the sensible reflects." And while I don't sympathize too much with wisdom, sometimes — even by tantrum — I'm stubborn enough, to the point of acting in complete disagreement with what I myself dislike, just to eventually be able to reflect weightlessly:

After all, why would there be a French Attention Deficit Association if the disorder wasn't even frequent there? Or why would a Facebook page (Hyper Supers — **ADHD** France) with more than 18,000 members, founded since February 5, 2002 with the Mission to Help People Affected by Hyperactivity Attention Deficit Disorder **(ADHD)?** Would the experts of the French Association of Attention Deficit in the absence of people with ADHD, be attending, producing scientific articles, providing informative services, and guiding hyperactive insects?

Other reports -- no less irresponsible and equally fanciful -- claimed that several young people would be using Ritalin (Methylphenidate Hydrochloride) in order to become more lit, and well-disposed to parties such as *Raves* and Carnivals. In one of these subjects, they even mentioned the case of a young nurse who claimed to feel yummy, beautiful, and with a sense of power — as well as experiencing a shiver as if preceding an orgasm — every time he took the drug. Another subject claimed to make use of the medicine before going out to ballads, ensuring that under the influence of Ritalin he already arrived at parties kissing everyone.

I confess —with the contradictory sarcasm of the seriousness of those who would confess something really important —that in the face of all these cases, I was ironically worried: or they would be selling me the counterfeit medicine, or that pill I was taking daily, for so many years, it would be any other remedy except that Ritalin with so many magical powers. First, because by pharmacodynamics itself, its substance causes much more a pathetic effect than excitatory. At least, it is how it works in my body the active ingredient of Ritalin that I make use of. According to that, indolent, with decreased sexual desire, xerostomia (dryness of the mouth), worsening of sociability, greater tendency to irritability, in addition to the effect known as "tunnel vision" (when the person holds so intensely in something, that ignores all other things and people around them), do not seem to be sensations of the nicest, nor so libidinous so for someone to want to go around buzzing with enthusiastic size.

As if enough were not much, or as if the much was not yet enough, time in another was reproduced, on numerous web pages that had nothing more useful to disclose, that same old news, outdated and already disproved for years: the image of a burlesque gentleman, illustrating the title: "Dr. Leon Eisenberg, the father of **ADHD**, said just before his death that **ADHD** is a fictitious disease".

Leaving aside, all incoherence inserted in the sayings that they make up of this news. After all, a father declaring that his own son would be a fiction invented by himself, it was at least something quite misplaced to already credit, in advance, so much truthfulness about the content of the news. However, whenever time was left to the setback of missing, I ended up not containing myself in replicating some of these sites. In one of these —through the space intended for criticism, suggestions and comments — I decided to give back to your columnist, a pharmaceutical and biochemistry consultant.

Initially, I stated that in translating the original text into German, she (or some other equally incompetent translator) had modified all the veracity of the facts: in what was actually said, at the place where it was said, when it was said, and by whom it was said. For example, the title itself does not match the truth, nor with the information reported by herself in the discussion of her own text: "Confession of deathbed of the inventor of **ADHD : ADHD** is a fictitious disease [...] At the age of 87 and seven months before his death, **ADHD's** scientific father stated in his last interview: **ADHD** is an excellent example of fictitious disease."

First, because the claim that Dr. Leon Eisenberg would have declared this would put the date of his utterance around February 2009. However, as for the documentation for putative quotation is provided in English, the statement that **ADHD** would be a manufactured disease, refers to an interview conducted on August 2, 2012 with Harvard University Professor of Psychology, Dr. Jerome Kagan. And with the title, Spiegel Interview with Jerome Kagan: What about Tutoring Instead of Pills? (What about Explanations instead of pills?), was it enough only a single answer

(1.2) of the interviewee to, at last and finally, disprove that news so plagiarized, lagging, recurrent and that filled the bag of any and all **ADHD** carriers.

1.1 Spiegel: Experts say that 5.4 million American children have typical **ADHD** symptoms. Are you saying that this mental disorder is just an invention?

1.2 Kagan: That's correct; it's an invention. Every child who is not doing well at school is sent to see a pediatrician, and the pediatrician says, "It's **ADHD,** here's Ritalin. "In fact, 90% of these 5.4 million children do not have an abnormal dopamine metabolism. The problem is that if the drug is available to doctors, they will make the corresponding diagnosis.

While another article -- not aired through the site but reproduced by *the Newspaper Der Spiegel* -- made it clear that Dr. Eisenberg at no point stated that   **ADHD** was an unreal disorder. In fact, he had said only that: *"The genetic predisposition of **ADHD** is completely overrated."*

Then, as serious as my bully impulsivity managed to curb all the momentum of my verbal irony, I presented to the then columnist, the link of a website, where people, much more reasoned than it, presented arguments (inconsistent, but who already validated more than all this unsubstantiated news) with intent to prove the absence of giraffes. They claim that these animals, when they appear in films, are mere montages, while those of zoos, at best, would be species of robots. And they consider idiots, all those who believe in the existence of the animal. Finally, I explained that perhaps the absurdity that was revealed to her in front of these people who did not believe in giraffes was as incoherent to me as those who do not believe in the veracity of **ADHD.**

However, I must admit that, immensely more ruinous than all this news deleterious, occurs when the discredit arises precisely from those people closest to their reality. As previously reported, in the book *Tendency to Distraction,* Edward Hallowell and John Ratey (1999) mentioned, including, among the first of the most common problems in the treatment of **ADHD**:

> Some people, especially important in life — father, mother, spouse, teacher, boss, friend—do not accept the diagnosis of **ADHD.** They don't "believe" in **ADHD** and don't want to argue about it. It's like it's against your religion or worldview. They make the person with **ADHD** feel a fraud or an impostor. This type of disbelieving response can undermine both the hope that accompanies the diagnosis and the treatment. Variants of the type are often heard: "This **ADHD** does not exist. It's just an excuse for laziness." [...] The important thing is information. Introduce the facts to the person. Stick to the facts, their sit-in to face superstition, rumors, told me, prejudice and misinformation. Try to avoid inflamed debates. It is common to use diagnostic objections to hide emotional issues. There may be anger from the diagnosed person. There may be resentments towards the person for all their mistakes and not if you wish that they escape easily with a diagnosis. They want punishment and so they are increasingly angry at the notion of **ADHD,** trying to make it fall into disrepute. In these moments it is better to stay with science, so stay with

the facts we have about the **ADHD.** At some point feelings of anger should be treated for what they are: anger in general stems from an annoying past behavior on the part of the person with **ADHD.** These feelings are perfectly understandable and valid. However, they should not be used to invalidate a correct diagnosis of **ADHD.**

I also confess — against all my willingness to omit that —the dismay over my condition, has never only been limited to **ADHD.** I have never even had a complicit perception of all the damage that a whole academic life with Dyslexia had cost me. Of the low school income, through the misunderstanding of almost everything I read and/or wrote. Triggering serious problems characterized in the precise or fluent recognition of words, decoding problems, and orthographic difficulties. As Willcut (2001) states, the presence of **ADHD** significantly increases the impairment of reading processing in dyslexic patients: reading requires a considerable level of attention to select relevant information and ignore less important stimuli. People with **ADHD** in comorbidity with Dyslexia have more behavioral problems, lower self-esteem, higher incidence of school dropout, and a worse prognosis when compared to the group with **ADHD** or Dyslexia alone.

> Dyslexia is the most common Learning Disorder (A), occurring in about 8% of school-age children. More conservative estimates point to the prevalence of AD in approximately 25% of children with **ADHD.** Both **ADHD** and Dyslexia are associated with multiple neuropsychological deficits, in particular with impairments of executive functions (WILLCUT, 2001).

I do not know if by the absence of self-pity that never incited my vocation to interpret the vitimist — or because for me it has always been given the role of understanding everyone's disorder around me. However, the prevalence of truth is that, without ever realizing the deep embarrassment that that kind of disregard about my condition caused me, on November 25, 2013, I received from a "person very close to my reality", an email with the link of an interview, as absurd and abstract as some mentioned above:

Indiscriminate use of Ritalin can cause 'genocide of the future', says pediatrician.

Indicated to treat patients with attention deficit and hyperactivity **(ADHD),** Ritalin has been indicated uncontrolledly in the country. Currently, Brazil occupies the world's second position of drug use, behind only the United States. In the case of children, who have the organism still in the growth phase, the risk is even greater. "There is a lot of talk that if the child is not treated, it will become a chemical or delinquent dependent. No given allows you to say that. So, you don't have proof that it works. On the contrary: it does not work. And what's happening is that the diagnosis of **ADHD** is being made in a very large percentage of children, indiscriminately," says pediatrician Maria Aparecida Affonso Moysés, a professor at the Department of Pediatrics at unicamp's Faculty of Medical Sciences (FCM). The expert says that if there is no stricter control over the drug, future generations could suffer considerably. "We run the risk of genocide of the future." Ritalin is a Methylphenidate, from the amphetamine family, and aims to improve concentration, decrease tiredness and accumulate more information in less time. It turns out that the drug can bring chemical dependence because it has the same mechanism of action as cocaine and is classified by the Drug Enforcement Administration as a narcotic. Adverse reactions to drug use take place throughout the body and, in the central nervous system, are more incisive. "This is mentioned in any book of Pharmacology. The list of symptoms is huge. If the child has already developed chemical dependence, it may face the abstinence crisis. It may also present outbreaks of insomnia, drowsiness, worsening in attention and cognition, psychotic outbreaks, hallucinations and risk committing even suicide. Data registered in the *Food and Drug Administration* (FDA) are recorded.

Disregarding the nefarious prognosis used as the title of the interview, initially, the slight oversight of the pediatrician in mentioning only the marketing name of one of the drugs, Ritalin, rather than citing them in allusion to its active ingredient, the Methylphenidate hydrochloride, which in addition to covering the trade names of other types of Methylphenidate available in Brazil — would provide readers with a greater understanding of their differentiation in dosages, from the manufacturers' laboratories, and mainly, in relation to its time of action:

a) Ritalin® 10 mg. (Novartis Laboratory): Short-acting methylphenidate, in effect, from 3 to 5 hours;

b) Ritalin ® LA 20, 30, and 40 mg. (Novartis Laboratory): Prolonged-acting methylphenidate, with an effect of approximately 8 hours;

c) Concerta ® 18, 27, 36 or 54 mg. (Janssen-Cilag Laboratory): Prolonged-acting methylphenidate, in effect, from 10 to 12 hours;

By declaring that the drug is "indicated to treat patients with attention deficit and hyperactivity (**ADHD**) — although it may, but should not consider as a serious misunderstanding — the mere omission of the term "disorder" preceding the expression "deficit", already in the use of vowel "and" in the interval of the words "attention" and "hyperactivity", it seems unaware of the existence of cases where the disorder occurs without the presence of hyperactivity. Because of this, even since 1994 the *American Psychiatric Association* (APA) adopted the term Hyperactivity Attention Deficit Disorder, with the use of the bar preceding "Hyperactivity" as a demonstration that the disorder may arise with or without hyperactivity, although hyperactivity is the symptom that defines this picture most. Also, in this same stretch, it also demonstrates not knowing that in addition to **ADHD,** Methylphenidate is used in the treatment of cases of Narcolepsy, and Idiopathic Hypersomnia.

Then, when it states that "Ritalin has been indicated uncontrolledly in the country. Currently, Brazil occupies the world's second position of drug use, behind only the United States." Even not to mention data, prognosis, percentages, statistics, estimates, lies etc. or any kind of resource ahead of their fallacies, as someone with a specialty is expected about what she says, yet she achieves the incredible feat of making serious numerical mistakes by the very dimity of what she does not know. Although between Set. /2011 and Oct./ 2012, methylphenidate consumption in Brazil showed a significant increase of 1,853,930 in the number of boxes sold, there are two antagonistic factors, but equally logical that pediatricians certainly do not know. Or if she knows — unlike the normality of those who know what they're talking about — she preferred to demonstrate her insipidity:

1º. Despite the large increase in the sale of Methylphenidate, if weco-found the data on the prevalence of **ADHD** in Brazil around 17 million people, even with all 1,853,930 boxes, about 30,000 patients would only be being treated with Methylphenidate in the country.

2º. However, it is impossible to know if there really is an excess in the consumption of Methylphenidate in the country, without knowing the amount of the drug being used for the treatment of cases of Narcolepsy and Idiopathic Hypersomnia, the percentage of people diagnosed with **ADHD** being treated with Methylphenidate, guessing (since it is not known) how many boxes are acquired illegally, being able to access the amount of Methylphenidate provided to the Health Unic System (HUS) (which are not accounted for in the studies) to only thus make the correlation between all these data with the prevalence of **ADHD** in the country.

3º. This all disregards that the interviewee completely ignores the aggravating factor of — unlike other countries — there is only Methylphenidate as a drug substance of choice available for the treatment of **ADHD** in Brazil. Which inevitably greatly enhances its consumption.

By vaguely mentioning, as you do during the entire text: "There is a lot of talk that if the child is not treated, it will become a chemical or delinquent dependent. No given allows you to say that. So, you don't have proof that it works. On the contrary: it does not work." Well...As for the excerpt in which the *pseudo specialist* mentions the risks of lack of control, claiming: "[...] if there is no stricter control over the drug, future generations may suffer considerably."

Subsequently, aside from the use of hypothetical expressions, when it states that the drug does not work, in addition to contradicting the numerous scientific articles available, usually in the academic environment when we affirm or disagree with something, we must present some kind of technical and/or scientific resource (research, articles, etc.) to substantiate what we stand for. She, unlike true experts, to support her arguments, does not even use *Wikipedia* as an allegation of its data collection source.

By saying that "Ritalin is a Methylphenidate, of the amphetamine family, and aims to improve concentration, decrease tiredness and accumulate more information in less time. It turns out that the drug can bring chemical dependence because it has the same mechanism of action as cocaine, and is classified by the *Drug Enforcement Administration (DEA)* as a narcotic", the interviewee expresses precisely the opposite of what numerous studies affirm:

the efficacy of Methylphenidate has its proven action in reducing symptoms of attention deficit, better performance of motor activities, reducing hyperactivity, controlling impulses, — and to the extreme setback of what it says at random— the use of Methylphenidate, of long-release types, even provide an inhibition of drug abuse.

Already about "reducing tiredness and accumulating more information in less time", or it suffers from some kind of mental alienation, or lacks a reasonable ability to understand some reality outside of her personal opinions. Due to ineptitude, ignorance or incompetence, the pediatrician cites entities with attributions that are not of their competencies. In the United States, the *Drug Enforcement Administration* (DEA) is not the institution responsible for classifying drugs. The DEA's mission is to enforce the laws relating to controlled substances, and to supervise organizations and/or persons involved in the manufacture and/or distribution of these substances. In fact, the *Food and Drug Administration* (FDA), a U.S. health surveillance agency, is responsible for classifying drugs and/or medications.

With regard to the analogy it tries to create between Cocaine, Amphetamine, and Methylphenidate, it is important to highlight that only two amphetamines are legally marketed in Brazil: Dextroamphetamine, and Methamphetamine. And although the three substances have similar Chemical Formulas:

(A)   Methylphenidate ($C_{14}H_{19}NO_2$);

(B)   Amphetamine ($C_9H_{13}N$);

(C)   Cocaine ($C_{17}H_{21}NO_4$),

They are totally divergent in relation to pharmacokinetics (route of administration, absorption, biotransformation, bioavailability and excretion). They are also distinct as the main chemicals (neurotransmitters) that interact, how they interact. And above all, they act in different regions of the brain. While Methylphenidate acts in the outermost layers of the brain, known as the cortical region (site related to memory functions, attention, consciousness, language, perception and thought), Cocaine and Amphetamine act in the *Accumbens Nucleus,* portion of the "reward system" (one of the main areas responsible for predisposition in chemical and physical dependence). Cocaine and Amphetamine are Monomania Oxidase Inhibitors (IMAO) promote increased availability of norepinephrine and serotonin in the synaptic cleft (space between two neurons). Methylphenidate, in turn, is a Dopamine Reuptake Inhibitor (DRI), however, in addition to not activating the "reward system" acts more in modulating dopamine levels than from Norepinephrine.

Roughly — propagated only by common sense — from which I presume to derive the non-existent knowledge of the pediatrician, it can be said that Methylphenidate works by what is usually called the "paradoxical effect", that is, it is a psychostimulant, but that has a contrary effect.

Even reproduced by journalists and/or non-specialized professionals, not to mention references, report scientific articles, or present any research that validates their lying statements, these types of libelous and alienating subjects - convey to readers a false idea that there may be doubts about the existence of **ADHD.**

Claiming that **ADHD** does not exist, as well as claiming that the drugs used for its treatment are "dangerous" beyond the explicit demonstration of ignorance, can be configured as a crime because it conveys wrong information on public health. Reproducing misleading news, while omitting hundreds of scientific data documenting the benefits, efficacy and safety of medicines used to treat **ADHD**, not only hinders and delays people's access to diagnosis and treatment, but also reveals bad faith, disengagement. to the basic principles of journalism and expresses one of the most perverse forms of discrimination against people suffering from mental disorders and / or disabilities: the Psychophobia.

The World Health Organization (WHO) defines Mental Health as a welfare state in which the individual is able to exercise his skills, manage normal stressful events in life, work productively and contribute to his community. A Mental Disorder, therefore, can be understood as a medical condition that alters this state causing impairment in the individual's overall performance. According to the Brazilian Psychiatric Association (BPA) it is estimated that more than 40 million people in Brazil suffer from some type of mental disorder. Thus, those suffering from Depressive Disorders,

Obsessive-Compulsive Disorder (OCD), Hyperactivity Attention Deficit Disorder **(ADHD)**among so many other mental illnesses begin to feel increasingly excluded, in the face of these types of prejudiced manifestations disseminated by the media.

On the existence and veracity of **ADHD,** it is worth noting that — in addition to being officially recognized by the World Health Organization (WHO) — **ADHD** is also validated by an International Consensus: scientific production published after extensive debates among researchers from different cultures, institution, and that they do not necessarily share the same ideas about all aspects of a disorder. According to the *American Psychiatric Association* (1994) **ADHD** is one of the best studied disorders in medicine, and general data on its validity are much more convincing than most mental disorders, and even many medical conditions.

Currently, **ADHD** is the most frequent reason among children and adolescents referred for care in specialized services. It is estimated that it affects 2.5% of adults, about 3 to 7% of school children (from 6 to 12 years old) worldwide, and in more than 68% of cases the disorder remains throughout life. According to the Diagnostic and Statistical Manual of Mental Disorders in its 5th edition (DSM-V), **ADHD** is more common in males than in females, in the proportion of 2:1 in children, and 1.6:1 in adults. The characteristics related to inattention have a higher incidence in females, while symptoms related to hyperactivity and impulsivity are more observed in males. The disorder also has high rates of comorbidities: in children with **ADHD**, more than 50% of cases arises with the presence of — at least — some other comorbid disorder, and approximately 10% of them, develop three or more comorbidities. Research indicates that among children, the most frequent are:

- Defiant Opposition Disorder — 40 %

- Anxiety Disorders — 34%

- Conduct Disorder - 14%

- Learning Disorders (Reading, Calculus and/or Writing) - 10 to 25%

- Tic Disorder — 11%

- Mood Disorders - 4%

Among adults with **ADHD,** comorbidities affect approximately 70% of patients — of which 97% have up to four comorbid disorders. Studies indicate that for every five adults undergoing treatment for some other disorder, at least one of them has **ADHD.** Among the most common comorbidities observed in adults are:

- Depression — 20 to 30%

- Anxiety disorder -20 to 30%

- Substance use - 25 to 50%

- Smoking - 40%

- Antisocial personality disorder - 25%

- Sleep disorder - 75%

In addition to triggering serious losses of productivity and motivation in academic, vocational activities, as well as a reduced ability to express ideas and emotions, instability in different types of relationships, impairment of execution memory, social retracting, negative effects of the image itself, etc. Hyperactivity Attention Deficit Disorder **(ADHD)** usually causes a series of impacts in the course of a person's life:

1) Adults with **ADHD,** regardless of the level of education, earn salaries significantly lower than adults without the disorder. The study showed that the difference is around $10,000 annually for individuals with higher education and 4,000 for those with only high school;

2) 25% of adults with **ADHD** do not finish 2nd grade against 1% of adults without **ADHD;**

3) Only 15% of adults with **ADHD** attend university against more than 50% of adults without **ADHD;**

4) Adults with **ADHD** less often complete a University;

5) Adults with **ADHD** less often get full-time jobs than adults without disorder. Item accounts for 17% of the $77 billion of projected losses in the study. Generating economic impact on society;

6) About 25% of students with **ADHD** present learning problems in any of these sectors: oral expression, comprehension, interpretation of texts and mathematics;

7) 30% of children and adolescents with **ADHD** repeat at least one school year, multiple repetitions occur in 21%;

8) 35% of adolescents with **ADHD** drop out of school, 45% are expelled from schools and 21% have classes repeatedly;

9) It is estimated that the emotional development of children with **ADHD** is about 30% slower than that of children without the disorder. For example, a 10-year-old with **ADHD** operates at a maturity of 7 years. A young 16-year-old driver with **ADHD** has a profile of decisions of an 11-year-old;

10) 65% of children with **ADHD** present challenge behaviors of authority such as verbal hostility and tantrums;

11) Children with **ADHD** are often victims of head trauma or polytrauma, accidental intoxications and ICU admission as a result of these medical complications;

12) Children with **ADHD** have a 3-fold higher risk of domestic accidents, 2 times higher than trauma, sutures and hospitalizations and 20% of them are responsible for serious fires in their communities;

13) Increased risk of pregnancy before 18 years of age and sexually transmitted diseases in young people with **ADHD;**

14) Young people with **ADHD** have a 4 times higher risk of causing accidents, 7 times higher than multiple accidents and with victims, and 4 times higher the incidence of fines (due to speeding and not respecting traffic signs);

15) Young people with **ADHD** are at higher risk of substance use, abuse and dependence. In a survey, tobacco use was reported by 50% of young people with **ADHD** against 27% of young people without the disorder, alcohol use 40% versus 28% and marijuana 17% versus 5%;

16) Separation or divorce occurs 3 times more among parents of children with **ADHD** than parents of children without the disorder;

17) 49% of children with **ADHD** have difficulties in relating to other children versus 18% of controls (children without **ADHD);**

18) 72% of children with **ADHD** have conflicts with siblings and other family members against 53% of controls;

19) 48% of children with **ADHD** have ease of adaptation to new situations against 84% of controls;

20) 18% of children with **ADHD** reported having good friends against 36% of controls;

21) 52% of children with **ADHD** need parental help in school tasks against 28% of controls;

22) 26% of children with **ADHD** need the help of parents to get ready to go to school against 16% of controls;

23) Comparative studies show that adults with **ADHD** have more often: drug addiction (or drug addiction), suicide attempt, divorce, unemployment, professional dissatisfaction and social misfit.

Celebrities with ADHD

ADHD is one of the most recurrence mental disorders on the planet. From poor to rich, atheist to fanatic and famous to anonymous: there are all profiles of carriers. To break some paradigms about the disorder (such as that it is believed that it prevents someone from being successful and efficient in what they do), see this list with some cases of famous people who own **ADHD**. You may know some cases, but for sure others will be very amazing! Check:

1. **Sylvester Stallone.** Yes. The great, eternal and legendary Rambo has ADHD!

2. **Magic Johnson.** The basket player considered the NBA's top point guard also has ADHD.

3. **Tom Cruise.** Being a (world-renowned) and successful actor with ADHD seems like an impossible mission to you? Not for Tom Cruise.

4. **Jim Carrey.** Jim's case with the disorder is well known around the world. The actor incorporates **ADHD** well with his clumsy and agitated style, don't you think?

5. Prince Charles. The first in line of succession and holder of the Prince of Wales titles in England also know on the skin what it is live with **ADHD**.

6. Einstein. Humanity's greatest genius is a very knowledgeable case of **ADHD**. It clearly shows that the disorder does not prevent anyone from – based on much will, encouragement and effort – achieving efficiency, prestige and recognition.

7. Walt Disney. As difficult as the disorder may be, Walt Disney is the perfect case that being **ADHD** has its advantages, including the free and creative mind (which contributed to the births of the brand classics of the same name as its creator).

8. Pablo Picasso. Picasso was eternized by his unparalleled works, but also leaves a little-known legacy of overcoming **ADHD**.

9. Salvador Dalí. Dali's eccentric manner accompanied the **ADHD** he had. It is further proof that the creativity of the carrier is giant, even forming, of an extensive list of artists who possess the disorder.

10. Caitlyn (Bruce) Jenner. The former transsexual athlete has already been hailed as "the world's greatest athlete" in 1976 during the Summer Olympics in the U.S. and has ADHD.

11. Steve Jobs. Jobs also have **ADHD** and is another case that proves the creative potential of many people with this disorder.

12. Danny Glover. The actor and activist also have the disorder.

13. David Neeleman. The Brazilian businessman, descended from Dutch and American, founder of U.S. airlines JetBlue Airways, Morris Air, Canadian WestJet and Azul Brazilian Airlines also has **ADHD**. Can you believe multi billionaire David has the same inconvenience as other persons with **ADHD**?

14. Adam Levine. Adam Noah Levine is an American musician. He is the lead singer and guitarist of the band Maroon 5. He also participates in the reality show: The Voice - United States. He is a world-renowned case of Attention Deficit Hyperactivity Disorder.

15. Howie Mandel. Howie is an American comedian and creator of the famous "Bobby's World". Coincidentally (or not), the creator of the **ADHD** icon character has the disorder.

16. Jennifer Lawrence. The lead actress of "The Hunger Games" and Oscar winner for best actress also know in her skin what it's like to have ADHD.

17. Justin Timberlake. With a very well consolidated career and unmistakable voice and waddle, Justin proves that a mental disorder like ADHD is not preventing enough for those who know what he wants and makes it happen.

18. Michael Jordan. This **ADHD** carrier is "nothing more, nothing less" than the guy considered the greatest basketball player in history.

19. Michael Phelps. The myth of swimming pools and greatest Olympic medalist in history, Michael Phelps, also has **ADHD**.

20. Michelle Rodriguez. Mayte Michelle Rodriguez is an American actress known for the films The Fast and the Furious, Fast Six, Resident Evil, Resident Evil: Retribution, Avatar, S.W.A.T. and from the famous television series 'Lost'.

21. Sir Richard Branson. Richard Charles Nicholas Branson is a British businessman, the founder of the Virgin group. Its investments range from music to aviation, clothing, biofuels and even aerospace travel.

22. Solange Knowles. Solange Piaget Knowles is an American singer, songwriter, DJ, dancer, actress and model. She's the sister of singer Beyoncé.

23. Will Smith. The disorder did not prevent him from becoming (nothing more, nothing less) than one of the most respected actors in the world, rapper, film producer, music producer and television producer.

24. Bill Gates. Who thought Jobs was alone representing the great world of technology business was wrong: the founder of T.I.'s best-known company, Bill Gates, also has **ADHD**.

25. Tracey Gold. American actress Tracey Gold is also the protagonist of our list of famous people with **ADHD**.

26. Usain Bolt. The fastest man in the world also knows what it's like to be known to be restless... And that led him to a huge number of Olympic medals!

27. Christopher Knight. Christopher is an American actor and closes this list of famous people with **ADHD.**

Testimonials from People with ADHD

I'm Like that

I knew it was different since I was a kid. I was born that way. Is it just me? I'd ask, ask, and there was no answer. I always felt like a stranger in the nest, a being from somewhere other than that. I didn't know, I just didn't know. I've always felt everything to the extreme. Love, hurt, friendship and all the feelings united in one. Sadness and joy smile and crying, curiosity and indifference. By the way, curiosity is what moves me. It's a curiosity from the simplest and most beautiful to the most unknown. It is a thirst for constant knowledge, even if it is not for an obvious goal. It is knowing, to understand, to answer the many "whys" of life.

I have doubts about everything. Past, present and future. Research, research and research and never settle for what people say just to shut me up. It's something like inexplicably loving the unknown. It is to be at the height of a right choice and abandon everything in search of the new. It's feeling alone in the middle of a crowd and feeling inserted in a context, being part of the world, even though I'm isolated in the room. It's fighting with my brother and stopping everything because I remembered that I bought him a medallion, in a church, on the same day. Deliver, explain how you use it and then fight again, but stop all over again because I didn't remember the reason for all that.

Is loving life!!! Wanting to live intensely every moment, and loathe the way people live, because deep down, deep down, I feel very different from everyone else. It's buying a gift for someone for no reason just because I'm happy, but not knowing why so much happiness. And when I try to remember why, I fall into deep sadness because I realize that everything is temporary.

I hate rules and norms, but I try to comply with them because I have respect for others. I talk to people I've never seen in my life, but sometimes I'll put a friend away talking to himself just because I remembered something through a word he said. And I run away because I had a lot of miraculous ideas about it, really magnificent.

With several thoughts at such a great and crazy speed that when I stop to write and organize everything, it's over. I've forgotten because in fact the sequences of thoughts are so intense that I lose myself in time. I lose the notion of time and space.

I can't rest in my sleep, so I get tired all day after, but when the night comes again for me to sleep, I get a total pike. It's so much energy, I don't know where it comes from and then I invent a lot of things to do and distract myself. I wake up wanting something, throughout the day I want another 50 and, at bedtime, I put everything aside because I already have a passion for a new idea. And I do everything I can to make it work, but then I see it didn't work out because I've given up.

I cry for the problems of the world, without at least solving mine. And I laugh in the middle of a serious meeting and soon I regret it because of the consequences. It's like I'm a child despite the responsibilities and missions to do.

I focus on a new subject as if it were the salvation of the world and I end up putting aside the chores that would save me the day. , without destiny and right direction. It's all very broad, the thoughts are broad.

In fact, no one around can understand me, and I don't even know how to explain. I can't do it. I lose friends for not being understood, but I understand all of them because I actually feel different and do not know how to explain why. But now I know why. It's all very confusing and I love being like this because if God made me with this little in my brain it's because I have a very different mission to accomplish and I just still don't know which one.

———————————————

By Flávia Mendes Gomes

Books on the Bookshelf

My room is a rat nest. All of a sudden, I get out of bed on a jump and put everything in its place. So, it's my heart, too. I try to get the books on shelves: one, for family people: daughter, husband, parents, brothers. Another, friends: those who are gone, those who are always close, those who have never been, but who love as much as others. Another, the acquaintances: people who come and go once or again, but who have made no marks. Another, the enemies: which ones? I have many of them. But I never know who they are. For me, everyone is good, they only make mistakes sometimes.

Then, after three days everyone is together on the same shelf, the labels got lost, I don't know who's who, who's from where. Wait a minute! That sounds like my office. (laughs).

My life is like this: everything has its place, but they change constantly. And then I don't know where they were from anymore, so people mix. Friends become family. Enemies, they become friends, and so you go.

It's confusing, but it's kind of good. With memories, that's the way it is, too. I hear one story, I remember another one, read one word No day is the same, because when he is born just like yesterday, I'm already different. Humor? I've got a lot. Bad mood, too... (laughs). I'm captivating with my talking way. But I'm tiring when I talk beyond the bill.

My stories are always the most fun, illustrated with gestures, sounds, mimes, etc. at least, I strive to the fullest. When I read a book, I enter the story: if it's raining in the tale, when I close the book, I run to close the windows, as if it were raining there, too. On the other hand, if the book is bad, I skip pages and go straight to the end.

Movies then... They're a problem: I hate watching alone, but nobody wants to watch with me. After all, my nickname turned out to be "cricritic", because each scene deserves a comment. Everything I do has to be the best. Being good, just, it's not enough for me. And if what you're doing isn't enough to be the best, wide in half and I don't finish anymore.

I love recognition and praise, but I love doing them, too. When I'm criticized or reprimanded, I always give an explanation. My fights are always fleeting. After all, I end up forgetting why I fought. I look at people and I know what they're thinking. Especially what you mean to me. I have lapses of imagination. I look at one thing, and I imagine a direct relationship with something else, which usually has nothing to do with everything has to have to do what and why!

I worry about what others think of me, so I do everything in the best possible way. I do five things at the same time now, when I get carried away in one of them, I dump all the others without remorse. I never forget God, I avoid asking, but I always do a morning. I'm extremely emotional. I'm crying just watching someone sing well at Raul Gil, can you? When I talk about people I like, they never have flaws, just qualities.

I wake up in the middle of the night to remember that I forgot my Uncle Kiko's birthday that was three days ago. Oh! But I remembered three dawn before the day, too. I love being philosophical, paradoxical. I observe graffiti drawn on the city walls and try to imagine what was going on in the head of those who designed it. What did he try to say? Am I crazy? Or, just disorganized ideas, really?

I guess I haven't forgotten anything, from I? So, the conclusion is for you to take it off.

Thatiana Nunes, 26 years old, publicist, married and mother of Giovana, with just 2 little years. Resident of São Paulo — capital, clinically diagnosed with ADHD, and never made use of Ritalin. At least to date, November 17, 2005.

ADHD Outburst — A Cry of Self-Knowledge

You know that child everyone thought was kind of "crazy", who did everything at the same time, with fleas in short, springs on his feet and a self-rechargeable stack?! Yes, it was me! I even think the character "Little Boy" had to be me, "Gisele — The Little Girl".

As a child, I only hung out with the boys because I always thought girls' games were boring and dull. And because of that I was always tasked with things like " *imp*" and " Male woman", but I never cared much for these things because I, even as a child, knew that it was not that and took in the joke or made me a plea.

I've always hated rules and I'm not much of a good thing about complying with them, especially those I don't agree with, or I don't understand why I follow them. During class I was always talking or up to some —tacks, gum, paper balls, tying laces of others and other gutters to colleagues or teachers. But I only took good grades and despite all this, the worst teachers (who all students hated because they were demanding) liked me. The director doesn't even talk... I lived on the board of punishment, and Loved it, because -- at least -- I'd have lunch and talk all afternoon with the main.

Curious to the extreme, I always wanted to know why things, how they worked and I have personal taste for different and unusual things. I could spend hours doing something, almost on another planet — usually doing things that other people thought was difficult — and for other things It distracted me from the noise of any pin falling to the ground. I've seen myself in a lot of trouble or embarrassing situations for it.

I almost always had the solution to some problem that no one could solve and wanted to put into practice, which always put me as a leader of group and room, even though I was "rebellious". But sometimes I get in the way of simple things, which my former boss says, "Swallow the elephant, but you choke on the mosquito...". My head is like a whirlwind of ideas... I only had one little problem: I kept forgetting things like important dates, commitments. I prefer a thousand proofs to a written job, because I always forget to do them.

For a "sleeper" child this scenario is even common, the point is that there is no way to describe a person's entire life in a brief text and the details of these and other situations only people who have **ADHD** can know. With all this childhood record, I got some stigmas: "She's not going to be anything in life if it goes on like this...", "Black family sheep. This one I don't know, saw..." and even my sexuality doubted that they liked the things boys liked because they were more active.

Although I'm already an adult, I still have many of these characteristics with "Rayovac", which I have been with since childhood. I took my life to date constantly dealing with "labels" and funny nicknames. I'm used to it and I know how to deal well with them being a humorous person and getting into the game. I've always felt a little or a lot: crazy, smart, forgotten, different, insane and fun. Almost everyone I know think I'm am fun, and they consider me a good friend for who I am and accept me like this, even though I can't understand myself most of the time. I understand that, since I can't even understand myself sometimes.

I found out about the **ADHD** by chance. I saw that a "virtual friend" had and, because I was curious, I researched what it was about. I read a subject from a medical site: " Attention Deficit Hyperactivity Disorder **(ADHD),"**Extracted from the book: ***Transform your brain, transform your life — by Daniel G. Amen.*** And as I read, I practically saw my life being described in every line of that text. Although long, I read in a few minutes (hyperfocus) and when I finished my hands were shaky and my head at a thousand an hour. I needed to make sure if I had **ADHD** or not before jumping to conclusions.

I researched more about the subject, Marcus Deminco was a great friend in this process, because he clarified to me several, doubts and appointed me a very ethical professional — Dr. Paulo, whom I also owe a lot, who, after consultation, diagnosed me as a **ADHD** of the functional type, since I can work, study and live with the situations of life, and so I do not need to take *Ritalin* and / or other remedies.

It is difficult for a person to spend his whole life being different, especially considering how humanity treats who or what is different, and at the age of 23 discovering a part of what makes him so different is shocking, but at the same time liberating. I think that's the feeling I had and I imagine I could have lived up to my last days on earth without ever knowing that I had **ADHD** and that others may be in worse conflicts than mine — since I was very lucky to know how to deal with the bad things of the **ADHD** and enjoy the good things.

I told my family, that it didn't show much surprise, since I was never very normal. And many of my friends don't believe or don't take seriously what I say about the **ADHD** and I have, when Marcus told me that He was writing this book on **ADHD** I was very happy, because being a book by someone who has **ADHD**, could pass an equal -- or at least similar -- that of other people who also go to these through same situations.

I continue to research about and exchange my experiences with others who have **ADHD.** With our fun, difficult and unusual situations, but above all: with the certainty that our life will never be simple, because we have come to give and see a special color to everything, because in fact, the life of a person who has **ADHD** is far from normal, common and common. And with these exchanges of experiences we can understand each other better and others to live better as well.

Gisele Reis, 24, Information Technology Administrator (IT). In addition to designer, coordinator of technological projects, dancer, counselor, commercial assistant and other things more... Like almost every good **ADHD** that has various affinities and abilities.

The ADHD Self

He always asked me if all others also lived with "thoughts a thousand"; if they kept thinking at any time; associations were made at all times with anything; if they had mood swings and emotions all the time; if they always lived "in the world of the moon". I began to understand my questions at the age of 18, when I knew how to be **ADHD** and I saw that the way i acted and lived was all "normal" for an **ADHD** being.

It is wonderful the cascade of emotions that you feel; the drastic and rapid change of mood; the countless amount of thoughts and ideas that passes through the speed of light through the mind; the inexplicable creativity that "appears out of nowhere" and takes over its being; love him passionately and madly.

It's horrible the fear of not working; insecurity; be aware that you forgot something, but not know what; feel like an imprestable, a useless, a excluded one that does not fit into society with its strict rules; suspect that your friends don't consider you so much you consider him.

Love so intensely that at all times one wishes to tell the loved one how he feels for him; always buy something that reminds you of the loved one, sometime lived, some comment heard, or merely some "crazy" association that only you understand yourself; think to have found the ideal person and perfect for you, the one to stay together until the end.

Love so simply and banally that you forget about that dinner scheduled for days; who greets the loved one in such a cold way that it generates the impression of no longer loving; that not of attention in the moments that the companion needs to speak.

The impulsivity of wanting to do something for yesterday; without taking a break to measure the real importance of the fact. But how many times and how many times in the middle of that "urgency" remembers something else very important, much more urgent than what is being made, but along the long road that leads to the place where the last to do will take place, the tireless mind diverts us to another door in order to accomplish something else.

Lie down in bed and often try to look for a "Stand By" button, a button to turn off your mind, to stop thinking and let sleep take over. The agony, because in the rush of everyday life when you get a little time at lunchtime to relax, the mind does not accompany the body, does not stop. And when you're getting to sleep, the alarm clock rings.

For me "mental journeys" are the characteristics that most alter my way of being and acting. Like, for example, when seeing a red pen remember a person, the perfume he wore, of complete conversations we had in his house, on the comfortable couch of his living room. And from the sofa arise a souvenir of the ride with the shopping shops, looking for new furniture home. And from the mall remember that movie you watched after you went wrong in a test. And from then on, until the moment comes when you realize the long time that was lost in the daydreams. It can also be dangerous as often in traffic focuses on a particular object and for a few moments lose attention in cars.

Being **ADHD** is living in the extreme. Either a man or a mouse. Do not stop using the mind to the point of generating the exhaustion of this, in which the only thing that is needed is rest. I can't imagine my life any other way. It is true that in many ways we have to keep controlling ourselves, so we don't make any mistakes.

I'm happy being **ADHD** and I don't think it would be funny if I stopped being.

____

By Filipe Ramo Barra

My name is Flavia, and my 9-year-old son Felipe has ADHD

At two years or even less, Felipe made mischief who looked funny and at the same time strange for his age. He was cheerful, had and has to this day an "enlightened" smile. When I was four, he went to school, and in less than two months, I had to take him out because he was always hurt and no one would explain to me why. I put him in another school. It was two years thinking that it was bad, unable to deal with more "active" children, until I took it again. We then went to third school, where he stayed for another two years. At this point, I felt embarrassed to go to school twice, at least, a week, to talk to teachers and principals about his behavior. Aerial, aggressive, messy, what was expected of me, because that was not my son. My Philip was and is a happy boy, good with life, radiant, and irresistibly charming.

I avoided jumping out of the car at the school entrance sign because I'd have to hear whispers and see glances directed at my son aggressively from the children's parents. Another school that didn't know how to handle the problem. The funny thing about this school is that he took more than fifteen warnings and thought it was fun, he came home happy, crazy to show, because even in the face of everything he went through, humor and joy always were constant.

In the next school, I spent all my son's problems, opened my heart with the psychologist of the institution, who proved super-receptive (until then, nor does he imagine that he would be have **ADHD**), that no child discriminate was against. At first, I felt good, but over time, I saw my son falling apart, sometimes falling into tears, self-esteem down there. I started looking at more and found out the school doing horrors. Instead of helping him, they took him out of the room (he was eight years old still in second grade) and took him to kindergarten class, where his four-year-old cousin studied and said that if he behaved like a baby, that's where he was going to stay. It was such the humiliation, that I had my son without the mood for nothing for a few days, just sadness. The main and school owner said no one liked him. Anyway, there were so many things, I saw him faltering, suffering, no friends. That hot joy, so soft, was disappearing... Needless to say, once again, in the middle of the year, I took him out of school and obviously I'm moving proceedings against it.

Finally, after this journey, I found a school where, once again, still afraid, I opened my heart. Then Yes, I found a school that welcomed him, when I first heard that my son could be a **ADHD.** I sought help, studied the subject and to this day

Diagnosed, today he has a quiet life. I do not see the **ADHD** as a problem, I see it as a light, a gift, something that being discovered at the beginning, being treated well and accompanied, provides a lot of peace to the **ADHD** and the family. Understanding made me calm down and find out the size of the treasure I have. It's hard still in a few moments but seeing it quiet is something that gives me strength and helps me take the calm and patience i need to understand and adapt to this life so "messy."

I believe that the **ADHD** leads a quieter life, being:

Surrounded by love, do not pamper;

Surrounded by care, without exaggeration;

Being heard, always;

Being understood daily;

Being helpful, useful, without being put aside thinking that with your fob ado way, things will fall, break, mess... The **ADHD** is a normal person like everyone else, but with a LIGHT that makes it special, just a smile to see!!!

By Flávia Maria Saldanha

I learned more from my kids than I taught.

At 27 I had my first daughter. The pink, quiet, sweet, doll named Camila. Motherhood was ravishing, a whirlwind of deep love, inexplicably greater than anything that the human being can one daydream of feeling something so wonderful that he soon wanted another child.

Gabriel arrived only 9 years after much waiting and asking God to get pregnant again. I can't put into words the outburst of happiness that took over me, my husband and my daughter, who always asked me for a brother. But life preached me some pieces... Camila has always been so quiet, organized, methodical, introspective, shy and cool, that I suspected there was something wrong there. A mother feels it. And I wasn't mistaken. Soon came the diagnosis of Asperger Syndrome (for the laity, the softer type among autism spectrum disorders — ASD).

But nothing in this world prepared me for everyday life and left me as bewildered as creating a hurricane named Gabriel. Before, we were a quiet, quiet, serene family. Soon things would be completely different and opposite... I realized I was in trouble when one afternoon, I put Gabriel to sleep. We were just me and him at home. My daughter at school and my husband at work. He was only nine and a half months old. I sat in the living room and watched TV.

Suddenly, looking at the ground, there he was, crawling, half crawling at my feet. I screamed scare! My first thought was that there was someone else at home who pulled him out of the crib. I ran into his room and was shocked by what I saw. He had placed close to the grill of the crib, the mischievous, on top of the straw, on top a teddy bear and on top a cradle protector. He made a ladder, went upstairs and then threw himself. He fell to the ground (I didn't hear anything) and he didn't cry. And he went to the living room to meet me. It was the first time I had the feeling that bigger surprises awaited me. And again, I was right.

He walked at 11 months. I moved everything, broke everything, went up, jumped, ran, screamed, burst, got up off the ground and kept running. He broke bones, teeth, tore nails, was always patched with stitches. I lived in the emergency room. He always had bruises so much he ran and got hurt. I stayed behind, attentive, trying to protect him, but he was more agile, faster, more disobedient and wouldn't listen to me. Came the idea of putting him in a school (in the nursery), because he was 2 years old and I believed that there he would burn his energy and have little friends.

Time or time again I appeared by surprise and saw his class sit, lined up, listening to the instructions, the school's stories... But... Where's Gabriel who was never there like the others? I soon spotted him running through the courtyard, with the desperate monitor behind him, flying from one place to another. It wasn't long before he was "invited" to retire. They weren't ready for such energy. I decided to put him in swimming. The teacher apologized and confessed not to realize... So, let's go to football. He paid attention to the ants, butterflies, the clouds of the sky, less on the ball and no one wanted him on his team, because he had no idea what he was doing there, since during the coach's explanations, he was scattered, running across the pitch. For everyone's relief, I decided to get him out of there. Let's try *taekwondo*. Discipline, rules, a rigorous and determined teacher... He asked for clemency two months later.

Gabriel was over classing, sticking the lines, couldn't wait and talk all the time. Good... We still have the sneakers. The balls flew in everyone's heads nearby. The racket also acquired wings and flew away. Again, he stuck lines, laughed too much, talked too much, ran too much and played less tennis... How about English? The school was the most commented in Sao Paulo, prepared only for children. The price of salting any pocket, but I wanted to try everything to occupy it, insert it socially.

Gabriel has always been fascinated by video game, mobile phone, computer. One day an English schoolgirl decided to take an electronic game and unhappiness did not allow my son to touch his toy. Frustration is not something he knew how to handle well... In five minutes, I was back in school, seeing by far the deep hate fults of the boy's parents, who had his glasses broken in his own nose, with a kick that according to Gabriel, he learned in a drawing... Again, he was "invited" to withdraw... He was already 8.

I'd jump from doctor to doctor. Therapy in therapy. Everyone said the same thing: **ADHD** with aggravating in impulsivity and Oppositional Defiant Disorder (ODD). I was driving my car with a shoe being thrown in the head by Gabriel. I'd swallow my lunch so I wouldn't take my eyes off him for a minute. I'd do anything running and distressed to come back close to him and watch him, afraid he'd get hurt. I was going to the bathroom with the open door. He took minute baths. He slept with one eye open and another closed. He supervised the pointy and cutting things of the house. I wash the windows with bars. I'd take the rugs off the floor so he wouldn't trip. I held his hand very hard when we were walking down the street. He always wanted to let go and run away. Going to the supermarket with Gabriel was asking me to stress out. He opened his arms and passed the shelves knocking down everything that came in front. What I put in the cart he'd take and throw away. Going to the movies was a waste of time. He didn't sit and talk loudly all the time.

In the restaurants, he ran and several times, he dropped the trays of the waiters with headbutts. I'd pick up fried chips and shoot the people who were sitting around us. Hanging out with him was a pain in the. I tried to punish you, talk, ignore, be very angry, promise rewards if his behavior was appropriate, but nothing... Nothing was fulfilled, he wouldn't even listen to me. The only thing that made him more focused was the Methylphenidate he took and that was a blessing in our lives.

He once told me that with the medication he could hear what people had to say, because he wouldn't stop a second to pay attention to anything... He spent seven years in high school, and it was seven difficult years. The coordination, the teachers, the board, the employees were excellent. They had touch, preparation, patience and a lot of skill with my son, but it wasn't like that with the schoolgirls and their families. I was always pointed out. Mr. Judged. Doomed, doomed. It was my fault that I didn't know how to raise that boy. At the time of the school break, it was reached to the point where my son had a security to accompany and watch him, since he was very ready in that short period of time. If I told the tears I shed, the nights I went through, the moments of despair, frustration, the fights with God, with the world, the people I eliminated from my user vivacity because they couldn't stand or understand Gabriel, the infinity would be too small to measure.

Nothing had prepared me for such a hyperactive son, so full of energy, so electric. I decided to put him in judo. Again, time and lost money. No one could take it. Although I often lost patience (I'm human), I defended my son with nails and teeth because I knew what **ADHD** was and had the real perception that he had no fault for being and acting like that. It's a neurobiological disorder. It's stronger than him, but much smaller than my tireless, unlimited, immeasurable and unconditional love for him.

The desire to help him turned me into someone else. I went to study, research, devour books. I participated in a thousand congresses, lectures, seminars, meetings, forums that discussed **ADHD**. He was still medicated, with a psychiatrist, with therapy, but he was still an atypical child. He came in causing it in the places; In high school all I could get away from the classroom was too restless to sit for hours...

At the age of 13, tired of trying so hard to have friends (because it was the way it was, I ended up scaring these "friends"), one day I caught him crying. He hugged me and told me he threw the towel. That no one understood him and couldn't stand to try to make friends anymore. That no one liked him. God knows what I felt at the time. I cried along with him, talking calmly and explaining to him how he was loved by all of us. I've always tried to raise your self-esteem, but there was no way. He was himself and never wanted to be friends with anyone again. For him only virtual friends, this he has many in online games, where he is a beast and quickly learned to read and write in English (better than in English).

One day I decided I needed to do more for him, and I looked for a regular school that had a special room and it was the best thing I did. Gabriel himself told me that he had finally realized that he was not the different "only" that there were others like him. Relaxed, never suffered *Bullying* again. He continues to hate his studies, saying that the school is nothing more than a prison, but is more adapted, with classmates who understand it and are similar to it. Today it is much better, less electric, more centered, more controlled. It's childish for your current 17 years. He has a real obsession with the computer (hyper focus) and his knowledge there is immense.

He's a beautiful boy, loved to the extreme for me, his father, his sister. I could never explain this rapturous love, which cheers me the days, which by seeing it makes my heart accelerate, which immediately brings a smile to my face. He and Camila are the reason for my life. A love for all eternity. I thank God for the privilege of having had two special children who taught me to grow up as a human being and to be a better person. I opened a Parent Association called *'Inspiree'*, with other mothers who also went through all this. Here in São Paulo I try to cherish parents with guidance and support that I did not find anywhere when my children were little. I, for some reason I don't know, have been chosen doubly and i am honored by this opportunity.

I also thank Marcus Deminco for the chance to leave my testimony here and be able to tell novice and young parents that there is a light at the end of the tunnel. That you need to chase knowledge, information and have a lot, but a lot of patience, because the rest only love solves.

Simone Alli Chair, 52 years old — São Paulo/SP. CEO of the Association of Parents Inspiree, President of the Kangaroo Institute (rare diseases), graduated in Social Work, popular defender, militant in the area of disability, but above all and all, Camila's mother, 25 years old Asperger Syndrome, graduated from the faculty of animation design and Gabriel, 17 years old, attending the year last of high school, with prospects of trying to design college in games, her passion. It has **ADHD,** with aggravation in impulsivity, Oppositional Defiant Disorder (ODD), and recently also diagnosed within the Autistic Spectrum. In treatment with a neurologist and a psychiatrist.

From destroyed self-esteem to Unstable Relationships: ADHD Can Destroy A Life.

I know very well what I've been through, and I'm still going to go today. I was born in 1971 and without understanding about **ADHD** and professionals who at that time did not exist (and there are few to this day) I had my whole life impaired. Without understanding why, even though I'm so smart on issues like creating and fixing things, because just in observing the functioning of things I'm able to disassemble and make it work again because they are situations that we have time to think, analyze the functioning and solve the problem without pressure, which usually does not happen in schools. And so, I grew up, with people always praising me for being creative, intelligent, etc.

But when I went to school, the thing was very different, I only stood out in the matters of fine arts and drawing and always as the best in the room, but in almost all other subjects I was terrible, but it was terrible not for being able to learn but for taking a while to understand and memorize how the other colleagues who took the subject faster, I was sad and always asking myself, "Am I stupid?".

In the classroom when the teacher asked, "Who didn't understand?" I kept quiet, because seeing that all the other schoolgirls had learned I was embarrassed and afraid to be called a donkey, but my low grades, and the need to paste colleagues denounced me and that's how I ended up being seen.

I'm sure if I'd had a different teaching, with people who knew about **ADHD,** things would be different and I would not have gone through everything I went through, because in my learning time respected and with a differentiated teaching methodology, I would have much more success in life, because I would have learned everything, even with all my lack of attention and difficulty in memorizing, because in my time I always learn everything, otherwise the consequence of this was to be phobia by classrooms and job even in job tests that make me sweat cold to this day.

On top of that, many are fears that reach a carrier of **ADHD.** Above all, with regard to relationships and future children... At least that's how it was with me, even though I struggled to forget, hoping that one day things would change, but unfortunately that's not how it happened. Sooner or later you end up realizing that all your fears are fulfilling gradually and the way you always feared.

I imagined having children and at school they would ask you about the subjects you never had the opportunity to learn as you should, due to your **ADHD**, your wife in disbelief about the disorder, not accepting and still saying that there is nothing wrong with you and if that wasn't enough, even buying a car became a distressing problem, when it should be a source of happiness, but it turns out not to be, because even being a good driver the difficulties in memorizing roads and understanding quickly certain street intersections me. It makes you fear going to far places, traveling with the car so don't even think! And so, I just use the vehicle to go to familiar routes.

My ex-wife charged me at the points where I couldn't go any further, and so I also created an almost phobia behind the wheel, simply for fear of new places and finally, the less you want the thing to get worse, come abandonment, she tells you that it doesn't give anymore , and the most frustrating thing about all this is knowing that it wouldn't have been like this if I didn't have the **ADHD**.

So the great need for early diagnosis, as I would now look for a partner with the same disorder, or when starting a relationship with a person without the disorder, would explain about **ADHD**, show stories that talk about it and hope that The partner understands and accepts my limitations, because with the help and not demands and criticism, can make any **ADHD** carrier overcome all the difficulties they may have in life.

––––––––––––––––––––

Daniel Rêgo de Aguiar (Salvador/BA), 44 Years Old, Security and graduated in ADM Assistant— Diagnosed with **ADHD** and In Treatment.

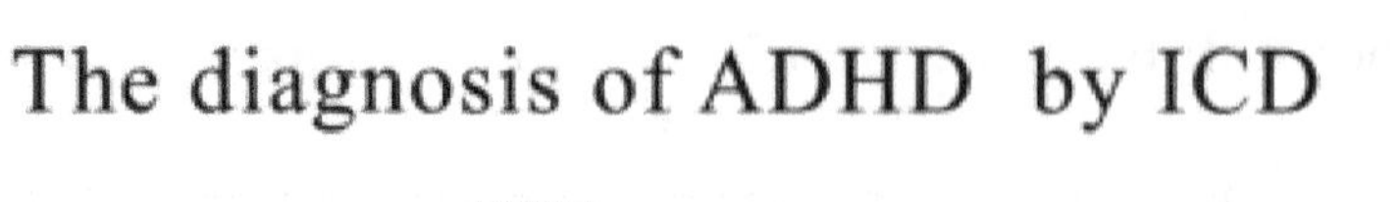

The diagnosis of ADHD by ICD

Published by the World Health Organization (WHO) the International Classification of Diseases and Related Health Problems, generally more recognized by the acronym **ICD** (International Classification of Diseases) — although it is not the most used instrument by mental health professionals in the preparation of diagnoses — also has its importance and purpose. The document provides codes that determine the classification and codification of diseases, and a wide variety of signs, symptoms, unusual aspects, complaints, social circumstances and external causes of damage and/or disease. For each clinical picture a single category is assigned to which a code corresponds, which can contain up to six characters.

Thus, the **ICD** serves as the main information vehicle in identifying trends and statistics of morbidity and mortality worldwide. According to the 10th edition of the International Classification of Diseases (ICD-10), hyperactivity attention deficit disorder (**ADHD**) is part of Hyperkinetic Disorders (F-90).

Hyperkinetic Disorders (F-90) are characterized by early onset (usually during the first five years of life), lack of perseverance in activities that require cognitive involvement, and a tendency to move from one activity to another without ending any, associated with a disorganized, uncoordinated and excessive global activity. Disorders may follow up from other anomalies. Hyperkinetic children are often reckless and impulsive, subject to accidents and incur more disciplinary problems for unpremeditated violations of rules than by deliberate challenge. Their relationships with adults are often marked by an absence of social inhibition, with lack of normal caution and reserve. They are unpopular with other children and can become socially isolated. These disorders are often accompanied by a cognitive deficit and a specific delay in the development of motricity and language. Secondary complications include dissocial behavior and loss of self-esteem.

Hyperkinetic Disorders (F-90) are subdivided into:

1) (F90.0) Activity and attention disorders;

2) (F90.1) Hyperkinetic disorder of conduct;

3) (F90.8) Other hyperkinetic disorders;

4) (F90.9) Unspecified hyperkinetic disorder;

According to the International Classification of Diseases (**ICD-10**) to diagnose a case of **ADHD** it is necessary that the evaluated person presents at least six of the symptoms of inattention and/or six of the symptoms of hyperactivity. In addition, these symptoms should manifest in at least two different environments, and for a period of more than six months.

A. With Predominance of Inattention

The predominance of **CARE** is characterized when the person presents six (or more) of the following persistent symptoms of inattention for at least 6 months, to a poorly adaptive degree and inconsistent with the level of development:

1. It often stops paying attention to detail or makes errors by carelessness in school activities, working among others.

2. He often struggles to keep an eye on tasks or recreational activities.

3. He often doesn't seem to listen when they're addressing his word.

4. It often does not follow instructions and does not terminate your school duties, household chores or professional duties (not due to opposition behavior or inability to understand instructions).

5. It often has difficulty organizing tasks and activities.

6. It often avoids, antipathizes or relutes to engage in tasks that require constant mental effort (such as school tasks or homework).

7. It often loses things necessary for tasks or activities (e.g. toys, school tasks, pencils, books, or other materials).

8. It is easily distracted by stimuli unrelated to the task.

9. It often presents forgetfulness in daily activities.

B. With Predominance of Hyperactivity and/or Impulsivity

It is characterized when six (or more) of the following hyperactivity symptoms persists for at least 6 months, to a poorly adaptive degree and inconsistent with the level of development:

B.1 Hyperactivity

1. It often shakes hands or feet.

2. He often leaves his chair in the classroom or other situations in which he is expected to remain seated.

3. It often runs or scales too much, in situations in which this is inappropriate (in adolescents and adults, it may be limited to subjective sensations of restlessness).

4. He often has difficulty playing or silently engaging in leisure activities.

5. It is often "a thousand" or often acts as if it were "in full swing".

6. He often speaks too much.

B.2 Impulsivity

1. It often gives hasty answers before the questions have been completed.

2. You often have trouble waiting for your turn.

3. Often interrupts or gets into other people's affairs (e.g., intrudes into conversations or jokes).

C. Criteria for both cases

In both cases the following criteria should also be present:

1. Some symptoms of hyperactivity/impulsivity or inattention that caused injury were present before 7 years of age.

2. Any impairment caused by symptoms is present in two or more contexts (e.g. at school, at work and/or at home).

3. There should be clear evidence of clinically significant impairment in social, academic or occupational functioning.

4. Symptoms do not occur exclusively during the course of an invasive developmental disorder, schizophrenia or other psychotic disorder and are no longer well explained by other mental disorder (e.g., mood disorder, anxiety disorder, dissociative disorder, or some personality disorder).

NOTE*: symptoms of inattention, hyperactivity or impulsivity related to the use of medications (such as bronchodilators, isoniazid and neuroleptic a catalyzed) in children under 7 years of age should not be diagnosed as **ADHD.**

The diagnosis of ADHD by DSM

The *Diagnostic and Statistical Manual of Mental Disorders*, better known by the acronym **DSM** is a manual for mental health professionals who lists different categories of mental disorders and criteria for diagnosing them. Prepared by the *American Psychiatric Association* (APA) currently represents the best clinical use tool to diagnose mental disorders-related conditions and has been one of the most widely used sources for mental health diagnoses worldwide.

In its 5th review, **DSM-V** classifies Attention Deficit Hyperactivity Disorder **(ADHD)** among Neurodevelopmental Disorders. Neurodevelopmental Disorders correspond to a group with beginning, usually manifested before the child enters school, being characterized by developmental deficits that result in impairments in personal, social, academic and/or professional functioning. Development deficits range from specific limitations in learning and/or controlling executive functions to triggering serious global damage in social skills or intelligence. There is also frequent the simultaneous presence of more than one disorder during the course of the individual diagnosed with some Neurodevelopmental

Disorder. For example, individuals with Autism Spectrum Disorder (**ASD**) often have Intellectual Development Disorder (**TDI**). While many children with Attention Deficit Hyperactivity Disorder (**ADHD**) commonly have comorbidity with some Specific Learning Disorder.

ADHD is a Neurodevelopmental Disorder defined by harmful levels of inattention, disorganization and/or hyperactivity-impulsivity. **(a)** Inattention and disorganization involve inability to remain on a task, appearance of not listening, and loss of materials at levels inconsistent with age or level of development. **(b)** Hyperactivity-impulsivity implies excessive activities, restlessness, inability to remain seated and/or in the same position and/or place. They also have meddling in other people's activities and inability to wait —symptoms that are excessive for age or level of development. In childhood, **ADHD** often overlaps with disorders in general considered "extremization", such as challenging opposition disorder and conduct disorder. **ADHD** usually persists in adulthood, resulting in losses in social, academic and professional functioning.

ADHD - Diagnostic Criteria (DSM-V)

A. A persistent pattern of inattention and/or hyperactivity-impulsivity that interferes with functioning and development, as characterized by **(1)** and/or **(2)**:

1. Inattention: Six (or more) of the following symptoms persist for at least six months to a degree that is inconsistent with the level of development and causes negative impact directly on social and academic/professional activities:

NOTE*: Symptoms are not just a manifestation of opposing behavior, challenge, hostility or difficulty in understanding tasks or instructions. For older adolescents and adults (17 years or older), at least five symptoms are needed.

---

a) He often pays no attention in detail or makes errors by carelessness in school tasks, at work or during other activities (e.g. neglects or lets details pass, work is inaccurate).

b) It often has difficulty keeping an eye on recreational tasks or activities (e.g., difficulty staying focused during classes, conversations, or prolonged readings).

c) He often seems not to listen when someone directs his word directly (e.g. he seems to be away with his head, even in the absence of any obvious distraction).

d) It often does not follow instructions to the end and cannot finish schoolwork, tasks or duties in the workplace (e.g. begins tasks, but quickly loses focus and easily loses course).

e) Often it has difficulty organizing tasks and activities (e.g., difficulty managing sequential tasks; difficulty keeping materials and personal objects in order; disorganized and sloppy work; poor weather management; difficulty in meeting deadlines).

f) It often avoids, dislikes or relutes in engaging in tasks that require prolonged mental effort (e.g. schoolwork or homework;

for older adolescents and adults, preparing reports, filling out forms, reviewing long works).

g) Often loses things necessary for tasks or activities (e.g. school materials, pencils, books, instruments, wallets, keys, documents, glasses, cell phone).

h) It is often easily distracted by external stimuli (for older adolescents and adults, it may include unrelated thoughts).

i) It is often forgotten in relation to daily activities (e.g., performing tasks, obligations; for older adolescents and adults, returning calls, paying bills, keeping schedules scheduled).

2. Hyperactivity and Impulsivity: Six (or more) of the following symptoms persist for at least six months to a degree that is inconsistent with the level of development and generates negative impact directly on social and academic/professional activities:

NOTE*: Symptoms are not just a manifestation of opposing behavior, challenge, hostility or difficulty understanding tasks or instructions. For older adolescents and adults (17 years or older), at least five symptoms are needed.

---

a) Often stir or batuca the hands or feet or writhe in the chair.

b) He often raises his chair in situations where he is expected to remain seated (e.g. he leaves his place in the classroom, in the office or in another workplace or in other situations that require him to remain in the same place).

c)   It often runs or climbs things in situations where this is inappropriate. (Note: In adolescents or adults, it may be limited to feelings of restlessness.)

d)   He is often unable to play or engage in leisure activities quietly.

e)   Often "does not stop", acting as if "with the engine on" (e.g. can't or feel uncomfortable standing still for a long time, such as in restaurants, meetings; others can see the individual as restless or difficult to keep up).

f)   He often talks too much.

g)   Often misses an answer before the question has been completed (e.g. ends other people's sentences, cannot wait for the turn to speak).

h)   You often have difficulty waiting for your turn (e.g. waiting in a queue).

i)   Often interrupts or meddles (e.g. get into conversations, games or activities; you can start using other people's things without asking or receiving permission; for teenagers and adults, you can step into or take control over what others are doing).

B.   Several symptoms of inattention or hyperactivity-impulsivity were present before the age of 12.

C. Several symptoms of inattention or hyperactivity-impulsivity are present in two or more environments (e.g. at home, at school, at work; with friends or relatives; in other activities).

D. There is clear evidence that symptoms interfere with social, academic or professional functioning or that they reduce their quality.

E. Symptoms do not occur exclusively during the course of schizophrenia or other psychotic disorder and are no longer well explained by other mental disorder (e.g., mood disorder, anxiety disorder, dissociative disorder, personality, intoxication or abstinence of substance).

Determine subtype:

- 314.1 (F90.2) Combined presentation: If both Criterion A1 (inattention) and Criterion A2 (hyperactivity-impulsivity) are completed in the last 6 months.

- 314.0 (F90.0) Predominantly inattentive presentation: If Criterion A1 (inattention) is met, but Criterion A2 (hyperactivity-impulsivity) is not completed in the last 6 months.

- 314.1 (F90.1) Predominantly overactive/impulsive presentation: If Criterion A2 (hyperactivity-impulsivity) is met, and Criterion A1 (inattention) is not completed in the last 6 months.

Specify whether:

In partial remission: When all criteria have been met in the past, but not all criteria have been met in the last 6 months. However, symptoms still result in impairment in social, academic or professional functioning.

Specify the current severity:

1. **Mild**: Few symptoms, if any are present, in addition to those necessary to make the diagnosis, and symptoms result in no more than minor impairments in social or professional functioning.

2. **Moderate**: Symptoms or functional impairment between "mild" and "severe" are present.

3. **Severe**: Many symptoms beyond those necessary to make the diagnosis are present, or several particularly severe symptoms are present, or symptoms can result in marked impairment in social or professional functioning.

Diagnostic Characteristics

The essential characteristic of Attention Deficit Hyperactivity Disorder is a persistent pattern of Inattention and/or Hyperactivity-Impulsivity that interferes with functioning or development. **INATTENTION** manifests itself through ramblings in tasks, lack of persistence, difficulty maintaining focus and disorganization - and does not constitute a consequence of challenge or lack of understanding. **HYPERACTIVITY** refers to excessive motor activity (such as a child running for everything) when not appropriate or rummaging, hitting or chatting in excess. In adults, hyperactivity may manifest itself as extreme restlessness or exhaustion of others with their activity. **IMPULSIVITY** refers to hasty actions that occur at the moment without premeditation and with high potential for harm to the person (e.g., crossing a street without looking). **IMPULSIVITY** may be a reflection of a desire for immediate rewards or inability to postpone gratification. Impulsive behavior may manifest with social meddling (e.g. interrupting others in excess) and/or making important decisions without considerations about the long-term consequences (e.g. taking a job without adequate information).

ADHD begins in childhood. The requirement that several symptoms be present before the age of 12 expresses the importance of substantial clinical presentation during childhood. At the same time, an earlier onset age is not specified due to difficulties in retrospectively establishing an onset in childhood. Adult memories of childhood symptoms tend to be unreliable, and it is beneficial to obtain complementary information.

Manifestations of the disorder should be present in more than one environment (e.g. at home and at school, at work). Confirmation of substantial symptoms in various environments is not usually done accurately without a consultation with informants who have seen the individual in such environments. Symptoms vary by context in a given environment. Signs of the disorder can be minimal or absent when the individual is receiving frequent rewards for appropriate behavior, is under supervision, is in a new situation, is involved in especially interesting activities, receives consistent external stimuli (e.g. through electronic screens) or are interacting in individualized situations (e.g. in an office).

Associated Characteristics That Support Diagnosis

Mild delays in linguistic, motor or social development are not specific to **ADHD,** although they are usually comorbid. Associated characteristics may include low tolerance to frustration, irritability, or mood lability. Even in the absence of a specific learning disorder, academic or professional performance is usually impaired. Inattentive behavior is associated with several underlying cognitive processes, and individuals with **ADHD** may exhibit cognitive problems in attention tests, executive function, or memory, although these tests are not sensitive enough or specific enough to serve as diagnostic indices. At the beginning of adulthood, **ADHD** is associated with increased risk of suicide attempt, especially when comorbidity with mood, conduct or substance use disorders.

There is no biological marker that is diagnosed with **ADHD.** As a group, in the comparison with pairs, children with **ADHD** present electroencephalograms with increased slow waves, reduced total brain volume in magnetic resonance imaging and possibly delay in cortical maturation in the postretirees anterior sense, although these findings are not diagnostic. In rare cases where there is a known genetic cause (e.g., Fragile X syndrome, 22qll deletion syndrome), the presentation of **ADHD** should still be diagnosed.

Prevalence

Population surveys suggest that **ADHD** occurs in most cultures in about 5% of children and 2.5% of adults.

Development and Course

Many parents observe for the first-time excessive motor activity when the child begins to walk, but it is difficult to distinguish the symptoms of normal behavior, which is highly variable, before 4 years of age. **ADHD** is usually identified more frequently during the years of elementary school, with inattention becoming more salient and harmful. The disorder becomes relatively stable in the early years of adolescence, but some individuals have worsened in the course, with the development of antisocial behaviors. In most people with **ADHD,** symptoms of motor hyperactivity are less clear in adolescence and adulthood, although difficulties persist with planning, restlessness, inattention and impulsivity. A substantial proportion of children with **ADHD** remain relatively impaired until adulthood.

In preschool, the main manifestation is hyperactivity. Inattention is more prominent in the years of elementary school. In adolescence, signs of hyperactivity (e.g., running and climbing things) are less common, and may be limited to more restless behavior or internal sensation of nervousness, restlessness or impatience. In adulthood, in addition to inattention and restlessness, impulsivity can remain problematic, even when hyperactivity was reduced.

Risk and Prognosis Factors

Temperamental. ADHD is associated with lower levels of behavioral inhibition, stress-based control or containment, negative affectivity and/or greater search for novelties. These traits predispose some children to **ADHD,** although they are not specific to the disorder.

Environmental. Very low birth weight (less than 1,500 grams) confers a 2 to 3 times higher risk for **ADHD,** although most children with low birth weight do not develop disorder. Although **ADHD** is correlated with smoking during pregnancy, part of this association reflects a common genetic risk. A minority of cases may be related to reactions to aspects of diet. There may be a history of child abuse, neglect, multiple foster homes, exposure to neurotoxin (e.g. lead), infections (e.g. encephalitis) or exposure to alcohol in the uterus. Exposure to environmental toxins has been correlated with subsequent **ADHD,** although it is not known whether such associations are causal.

Genetic and physiological. ADHD is frequent in first-degree biological relatives with the disorder. The heritability of **ADHD** is substantial. While specific genes have been correlated with the disorder, they do not constitute necessary or sufficient causal factors. Visual and auditory deficiencies, metabolic abnormalities, sleep disorders, nutritional deficiencies and epilepsy should be considered possible influences on **ADHD** symptoms.

ADHD is not associated with specific physical characteristics, although lower physical abnormalities rates (e.g., hypertelorism, rather arched palate, low ear implantation) may be relatively increased. Subtle motor delays and other mild neurological signs may occur. Note that lack of manner and comorbid engine delays should be coded separately (e.g. coordination development disorder).

Course modifiers. Patterns of family interaction early childhood probably do not cause **ADHD,** although they may influence their course or contribute to the secondary development of conduct problems.

Diagnostic Issues Related to Culture

Regional differences in **ADHD** prevalence rates seem mainly attributable to different diagnostic and methodological practices. However, there may also be cultural variations in terms of attitudes or interpretations about child behavior. Clinical identification rates in the United States for African American and Latin populations tend to be lower than for white populations. Symptom scores by informants may be influenced by the child's and informant's cultural group, suggesting that culturally appropriate practices are relevant in the evaluation of **ADHD.**

Diagnostic Issues Related to Gender

ADHD is more frequent in males than in females in the general population, with a ratio of about 2:1 in children and 1.6:1 in adults. Women are more likely to present themselves primarily with inattention characteristics compared to males.

Functional Consequences of ADHD

ADHD is associated with reduced school performance and academic success, social rejection and, in adults, worse performances, success and attendance in the professional field and the higher probability of unemployment, as well as high levels of interpersonal conflict. Children with **ADHD** are significantly more likely than their peers to develop conduct disorder in adolescence and antisocial personality disorder in adulthood, thereby increasing the likelihood of substance use and imprisonment disorders. The subsequent risk for posterior substance use disorders is high, especially when conduct disorder or antisocial personality disorder develops. Individuals with **ADHD** are more likely to suffer injuries than their peers. Traffic accidents and violations are more frequent in drivers with the disorder. There may be increased probability of obesity among individuals with **ADHD.**

Variable or inadequate self-determination to perform tasks that require prolonged effort is often interpreted by others, such as laziness, irresponsibility or lack of cooperation. Family relationships can be characterized by discord and negative interactions.

Relationships with peers are usually troubled due to rejection by those, neglect or taunts in relation to the individual with **ADHD.** On average, people with the disorder achieve lower schooling, less professional success and reduced intellectual scores compared to their peers, although there is great variability. In its severe form, the disorder is markedly harmful, affecting social, family and school/professional adaptation.

Academic deficits, school problems and neglect by colleagues tend to be mainly associated with high symptoms of inattention, while rejection by colleagues and, to a lesser extent, accidental injuries are more prominent with marked symptoms hyperactivity or impulsivity.

Differential Diagnosis

Defiant Opposition Disorder (TOD). Individuals with challenging opposition disorder can resist professional or school tasks that require self-determination because they resist conforming to the demands of others. His behavior is characterized by negativity, hostility and challenge. Such symptoms should be differentiated from aversion to school or to high-mental requirements tasks caused by difficulty in maintaining prolonged mental exertion, forgetting guidance and impulsivity that characterizes individuals with **ADHD.** A complicating differential diagnosis pain is the fact that some individuals with **ADHD** may develop secondary opposition attitudes towards such tasks and thus devalue their importance.

Intermittent Explosive Disorder (TEI). **ADHD** and intermittent explosive disorder share high levels of impulsive behavior. However, individuals with intermittent explosive disorder present important aggressiveness directed to others, which is not characteristic of **ADHD,** and have no problems keeping attention as seen in **ADHD.** In addition, intermittent explosive disorder is rare in childhood. Intermittent explosive disorder can be diagnosed in the presence of **ADHD.**

Other Neurodevelopmental Disorders. Increased motor activity that may occur in **ADHD** should be differentiated from repetitive motor behavior that characterizes stereotyped movement disorder and some cases of autism spectrum disorder. In stereotyped movement disorder, motor behavior is usually fixed and repetitive (e.g., shaking the body, biting itself), while restlessness and agitation in **ADHD** are usually generalized and not characterized by repetitive stereotyped movements. No; Tourette disorder, multiple and frequent tics can be confused with the widespread restlessness of **ADHD.** There may be a need for prolonged observation in order to distinguish between restlessness and multi-tic attacks.

Specific Learning Disorder (ASAs). Children with a specific learning disorder may seem unattentive due to frustration, lack of interest or limited capacity. Inattention, however, in people with a specific learning disorder, but without **ADHD,** does not cause harm outside of academic work.

Intellectual Disability (Intellectual Development Disorder). ADHD symptoms are common among children placed in academic environments unsuitable for their intellectual capacity. In such cases, symptoms are not evident during non-academic tasks. A diagnosis of **ADHD** in intellectual disability requires that inattention or hyperactivity be excessive for mental age.

Autism Spectrum Disorder (ASAs). Individuals with **ADHD** and those with autism spectrum disorder exhibit inattention, social dysfunction and difficult-to-manage behavior. Social dysfunction and peer rejection found in people with **ADHD** should be differentiated from the lack of social involvement, isolation and indifference to facial and tone communication cues found in individuals with autism spectrum disorder. Children with autism spectrum disorder may have rabies attacks due to the inability to tolerate changes in the course of events expected by them. In contrast, children with **ADHD** can misbehave or have an attack of anger during some major transition due to impulsivity or unsatisfactory self-control.

Reactive Attachment Disorder (ART). Children with reactive attachment disorder may present social disinhibition, but not the complete set of **ADHD** symptoms, exhibiting other characteristics such as absence of lasting relationships, which are not characteristic of **ADHD.**

Anxiety Disorders. **ADHD** shares symptoms of inattention with anxiety disorders. Individuals with **ADHD** are inattentive because of their attraction to external stimuli, new activities or predilection for pleasant activities. This is different from the inattention due to concern and rumination found in anxiety disorders. Agitation can be found in anxiety disorders. In **ADHD,** however, the symptom is not associated with concern and rumination.

Depressive Disorders. Individuals with depressive disorders may present with inability to concentrate. However, the difficulty of concentration in mood disorders is prominent only during a depressive episode.

Bipolar Disorder. Individuals with bipolar disorder may have increased activity, difficulty concentrating and increased impulsivity. These characteristics, however, are episodic, occurring for several days at a time. In bipolar disorder, increased impulsivity or inattention is accompanied by high mood, grandeur and other specific bipolar characteristics. Children with **ADHD** may present important mood swings in the same day; this lability is different from a manic episode, which should last four days or more to be a clinical indicator of bipolar disorder, even in children. Bipolar disorder is rare in pre-adolescents, even when severe irritability and rabies are prominent, while **ADHD** is common among children and adolescents who have excessive rabies and irritability.

Disruptive Mood Dysregulation Disorder. Disruptive mood deregulation disorder is characterized by pervasive irritability and frustration intolerance, but impulsivity and disorganized attention are not essential aspects. Most children and adolescents with the disorder, however, have symptoms that also meet criteria for **ADHD,** which should be diagnosed separately.

Substance Use Disorder (SUD). Differentiating **ADHD** from substance use disorders may be a problem if the first presentation of **ADHD** symptoms occurs after the onset of abuse or frequent use. Clear evidence of **ADHD** prior to problematic substance use, obtained through informants or previous records, may be essential for differential diagnosis.

Personality Disorders. In adolescents and adults, it can be difficult to differentiate **ADHD** from *Borderline personality* disorders, narcissist and other personality disorders. All of these tend to share characteristics of disorganization, social intrusion, emotional deregulation and cognitive deregulation. **ADHD,** however, is not characterized by fear of abandonment, self-injury, extreme ambivalence or other characteristics of personality disorders. There may be a need for prolonged observation, interviews with informants or detailed history to distinguish impulsive, socially intrusive or inadequate behavior from narcissistic, aggressive or dominating behavior in order to make this differential diagnosis.

Psychotic Disorders. ADHD is not diagnosed if symptoms of inattention and hyperactivity occur exclusively during the course of a psychotic disorder.

Symptoms of drug-induced ADHD. Symptoms of inattention, hyperactivity or impulsivity attributable to the use of medications (e.g. bronchodilators, isoniazid, neuroleptics [resulting in akathisia], thyroid replacement therapy) are diagnosed as disorder for the use of another substance (or unknown substance) or disorder related to another substance (or unknown substance not specified).

Neurocognitive Disorders. It is not known whether Early Major Neurocognitive Disorder (dementia) and/or Mild Neurocognitive Disorder are associated with **ADHD,** although similar clinical characteristics may often present. These conditions are differentiated from **ADHD** by its late onset.

Comorbidity

In clinical environments, comorbid disorders are frequent in individuals whose symptoms meet criteria for **ADHD.** In the general population, Defiant Opposition Disorder (TOD) is comorbid with **ADHD** in about half of the children with the combined presentation and in about a quarter of those with the predominantly inattentive presentation. Conduct Disorder is comorbid with **ADHD** in approximately a quarter of children and adolescents with combined presentation, depending on age and environment.

Most children and adolescents with Disruptive Mood Deregulation Disorder have symptoms that also meet criteria for **ADHD;** a smaller percentage of children with **ADHD** have symptoms that meet criteria for Disruptive Mood Deregulation Disorder. Specific Learning Disorder (ASD) is commonly comorbid with **ADHD*** Anxiety Disorders and Major Depressive Disorder (TDM) occur in a minority of individuals with **ADHD,** although more frequently than in the general population. Intermittent Explosive Disorder (TEI) occurs in a minority of adults with **ADHD,** although with rates above population levels.

Although substance abuse disorders are relatively more frequent among adults with **ADHD** in the general population, only one minority of them are present. In adults, Antisocial Personality Disorder (TPA) and other personality disorders can be comorbid with **ADHD.** Other disorders that may be comorbid with **ADHD** include Obsessive-Compulsive Disorder (OCD), Tic Disorders, and Autism Spectrum Disorder (ASD).

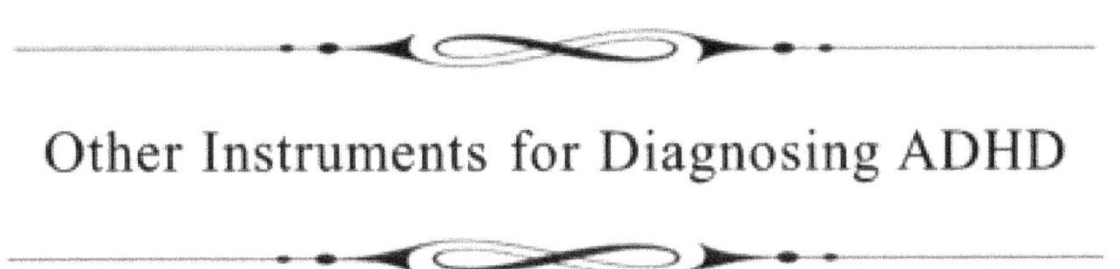

Other Instruments for Diagnosing ADHD

The evaluation process for the diagnosis of Attention Deficit/Hyperactivity Disorder **(ADHD)** should be carried out through a thorough clinical investigation, contemplating all patient history. However, the more careful this evaluation is performed in relation to the use of instrumental resources, the lower the possibility of making a misunderstanding in the diagnosis. An assessment that — in addition to providing an accurate diagnosis — is able to point out the presence of comorbid disorders, analyzing a perspective on the harmful and misfit functioning of the subject, will also provide a better choice related to the more efficient techniques and/or strategies to be used during their treatment. Thus, favoring the prognosis of the individual.

Thus, although the characteristics present in the International Classification of Diseases **(ICD)** and, above all, the Diagnostic Criteria described in the Diagnostic and Statistical Manual of Mental Disorders **(DSM)** are considered as the most reliable and consistent instruments to assist in the diagnosis process of **ADHD,** there is a wide variety of tests, scales and other psychological instruments that may, and should be used in order to corroborate the accuracy in the evaluation process and diagnosis of Attention Deficit Hyperactivity Disorder **(ADHD).**

SNAP-IV — For ADHD Diagnosis in Children and Adolescents

Public domain tool, the Swanson Nolan and Pelham-IV Questionnaire, or simply SNAP-IV is an easy-to-use questionnaire, was developed from the same criteria present in **DSM** to assess the symptoms of Attention Deficit Hyperactivity Disorder (ADHD) in children and adolescents. Because the characteristics of **ADHD** usually manifest themselves in different contexts, this questionnaire can also be completed by parents and/or teachers.

How to Use

For each of the **18** sentences described below choice and mark one of the **4** answer options that best corresponds to the child or adolescent evaluated.

1. You cannot pay much attention to detail or make mistakes for carelessness in schoolwork or chores.

( ) Not a little
( ) Just a little
( ) Quite
( ) Too much

2. You have difficulty keeping an eye on leisure tasks or activities.

( ) Not a little
( ) Just a little
( ) Quite

() Too much

3. You don't seem to be listening when you talk to him directly.

() Not a little
() Just a little
() Quite
() Too much

4. Do not follow instructions to the end and does not terminate school duties, tasks or obligations.

() Not a little
() Just a little
() Quite
() Too much

5. Have difficulty organizing tasks and activities.

() Not a little
() Just a little
() Quite
() Too much

6. Avoids, dislikes or engages against will in tasks that require prolonged mental effort.

() Not a little
() Just a little
() Quite
() Too much

7. Loses things necessary for activities (e.g. toys, school duties, pencils or books).

( ) Not a little
( ) Just a little
( ) Quite
( ) Too much

8. Get distracted by external stimuli.

( ) Not a little
( ) Just a little
( ) Quite
( ) Too much

9. It is forgotten in day-to-day activities.

( ) Not a little
( ) Just a little
( ) Quite
( ) Too much

10. Stir with your hands, feet or stir in the chair.

( ) Not a little
( ) Just a little
( ) Quite
( ) Too much

11. You leave the place in the classroom or in other situations where you are expected to sit (a).

( ) Not a little
( ) Just a little

( ) Quite
( ) Too much

12. Runs from side to side or climbs things in inappropriate situations.

( ) Not a little
( ) Just a little
( ) Quite
( ) Too much

13. Demonstrates difficulty in playing or engaging in leisure activities in a quiet way.

( ) Not a little
( ) Just a little
( ) Quite
( ) Too much

14. Not quiet or often is "a thousand per hour".

( ) Not a little
( ) Just a little
( ) Quite
( ) Too much

15. You talk too much.

( ) Not a little
( ) Just a little
( ) Quite
( ) Too much

16. Answer questions hastily before they are even completed.

( ) Not a little
( ) Just a little
( ) Quite
( ) Too much

17. Finds it difficult to wait for your turn.

( ) Not a little
( ) Just a little
( ) Quite
( ) Too much

18. Stop others or intrude in conversations, games, etc.

( ) Not a little
( ) Just a little
( ) Quite
( ) Too much

How to Evaluate

1. If at least 6 items were marked as **QUITE** or **TOO MUCH** from 1 to 9 = there are more symptoms of inattention than expected for a child or adolescent.

2. If at least 6 items were marked as **QUITE** or **TOO MUCH** from 10 to 18 = there are more symptoms of hyperactivity and impulsivity than expected for a child or adolescent.

IMPORTANT: You cannot diagnose **ADHD** only with criterion A. Therefore, to consider the diagnosis see below the other criteria that are also needed.

Criterion A: Symptoms (seen above)

Criterion B: Some of these symptoms should be present before 7 years of age.

Criterion C: There are problems caused by the above symptoms in at least 2 different contexts (e.g. at school, at work, social life and at home).

Criterion D: There are obvious problems in school, social or family life due to symptoms.

Criterion E: If there is any other problem (such as depression, mental deficiency, psychosis, etc.), symptoms cannot be attributed exclusively to it.

ASRS-18 - For the Diagnosis of ADHD in Adults

The Adult Self-Report Scale (ASRS-18) is an important tool to aid in the diagnosis of **ADHD** in adults. The scale was developed by researchers in collaboration with the World Health Organization (WHO) and validated for the Portuguese language in 2006. Considering that certain symptoms appear more strongly in specific environments such as work, at home or leisure, the scale is also recommended for it to be filled both by the patient and his/her family members, co-workers and/or friends.

The scale has 18 items that contemplate the symptoms present in **Criterion A** of the **DSM.** However, modified and adapted to the context of adult life. And it offers 5 different scores for each frequency response option:

1. **Never = 0 Points**
2. **Rarely = 1 Point**
3. **Sometimes = 2 Points**
4. **Often = 3 Points**
5. **Very Often = 4 Points**

How to Use

Answer the questions below according to the score the frequency answer options that best represent how the person evaluated felt and/or behaved in the last six months.

PART A

1. How often do you make mistakes for lack of attention when you have to work on a boring or difficult project?

( ) Never

( ) Rarely

( ) Sometimes

( ) Often

( ) Very Often

2. How often do you have difficulty keeping an eye out when you are doing a boring or repetitive job?

( ) Never

( ) Rarely

( ) Sometimes

( ) Often

( ) Very Often

3. How often do you have difficulty focusing on what people say, even when they are talking directly to you?

( ) Never

( ) Rarely

( ) Sometimes

( ) Often

( ) Very Often

4. How often do you leave a project in half after you have already made the most difficult parts?

( ) Never

( ) Rarely

( ) Sometimes

( ) Often

( ) Very Often

5. How often do you have difficulty doing a job that requires organization?

( ) Never

( ) Rarely

( ) Sometimes

( ) Often

( ) Very Often

6. When you need to do something that requires a lot of concentration, with what frequência you avoid or postpone the beginning?

( ) Never

( ) Rarely

( ) Sometimes

( ) Often

( ) Very Often

7. How often do you put things out of place or have difficulty finding things at home or at work?

( ) Never

( ) Rarely

( ) Sometimes

( ) Often

( ) Very Often

8. How often do you get distracted by aividades or noise around you?

( ) Never

( ) Rarely

( ) Sometimes

( ) Often

( ) Very Often

9. How often do you have difficulty remembering appointments or obligations?

( ) Never

( ) Rarely

( ) Sometimes

( ) Often

( ) Very Often

PART B

1. How often do you keep moving in the chair or shaking your hands or feet when you need to sit (a) for a long time?

( ) Never

( ) Rarely

( ) Sometimes

( ) Often

( ) Very Often

2. How often do you get up from the chair in meetings or in other situations where you should sit (a)?

( ) Never

( ) Rarely

( ) Sometimes

( ) Often

( ) Very Often

3. How often do you feel restless (a) or agitated(a)?

( ) Never

( ) Rarely

( ) Sometimes

( ) Often

( ) Very Often

4. How often do you have difficulty settle down and relax when you have free time?

( ) Never

( ) Rarely

( ) Sometimes

( ) Often

( ) Very Often

5. How often do you feel too active and needing to do things, like you're "with an engine turned on"?

( ) Never

( ) Rarely

( ) Sometimes

( ) Often

( ) Very Often

6. How often do you get too much falanin social situations?

( ) Never

( ) Rarely

( ) Sometimes

( ) Often

( ) Very Often

7. When you're talking, how often do you catch yourself by finishing people's sentences before them?

( ) Never

( ) Rarely

( ) Sometimes

( ) Often

( ) Very Often

8. How often do you have difficulty waiting in situations where each one has his turn?

( ) Never

( ) Rarely

( ) Sometimes

( ) Often

( ) Very Often

9. How often do you interrupt others when they are busy?

( ) Never

( ) Rarely

( ) Sometimes

( ) Often

( ) Very Often

How to Evaluate

If the items of inattention of part A (1 to 9) and/or the items of hyperactivity-impulsivity of part B (1 to 9) have several answers marked **OFTEN** or **VERY OFTEN** there is a great chance that the evaluated person is carrier that of **ADHD** (at least 4 in each of the parts).

IMPORTANT: cannot diagnose **ADHD** only with the symptoms shown in the table. To consider the diagnosis see below the other criteria that are also required.

Criterion A: Symptoms (seen in the table above)

Criterion B: Some of these symptoms should be present from an early age (up to 12 years).

Criterion C: There are problems caused by the above symptoms in at least 2 different contexts (e.g. at work, social life, college and marital or family relationships).

Criterion D: There are obvious problems due to symptoms.

Criterion E: If there is the presence of any other disorder (such as depression, mental deficiency, psychosis, etc.), symptoms cannot be attributed exclusively to it.

NOTE*: The American study that originated the creation of ASRS-18 suggests that a score above 24 is considered as a strong indication for the presence of **ADHD** in adults. However, it is essential to confirm attested by a specialist, considering that many of the symptoms described in the scale may be associated with other comorbidities related to **ADHD** and/or other psychopathological conditions.

Preliminary Assessment Criteria for ADHD in Adults

This test is based on the list of symptoms that characterize Attention Deficit Hyperactivity Disorder (**ADHD**) in its adult manifestation. However, its assessment should only be considered as a secondary resource for the indication of **ADHD**.

How to Use

Check in the table below, the options that best refer to the person evaluated. In the end, the more alternatives are marked, the greater the probability of the presence of **ADHD**.

Inattentive Type

(1) Pay little attention to detail and usually makes mistakes due to lack of attention.

(2) You have trouble concentrating when watching a lecture, reading a book, etc.

(3) Sometimes you don't seem to hear when they're being directed at you, or in a conversation you end up paying attention to other things.

(4) He has difficulty following the instructions (not because of inability to understand them), always preferring to do his tasks "in his own way", in "his time", often leaving them unfinished.

(5) Difficulty organizing your time to do something or plan something in advance.

(6) Reluctance to do or initiate tasks that require mental and constant effort for a long time.

(7) Loses objects and/or forgets names, appointments, dates.

(8) Easily distract yourself with things around you or even with your own thoughts, often appearing to "dream awake".

(9) It often presents forgetfulness in its daily activities.

It is necessary that the person has 5 or more of the above symptoms, in order to be more likely to diagnose ADHD of the Inattentive Type.

Hyperactive / Impulsive Type

(1) The feet, hands or stirs in the chair incessantly.

(2) You have difficulty sitting (a) in situations where this is expected.

(3) He feels unable to relax, rest, the musculature is usually tense and is always in search of something to do.

(4) He has difficulty staying silent in leisure activities.

(5) It seems to be powered by an "electric" engine, as it is always, the "thousand per hour".

(6) Talk, eat, buy or work too hard.

(7) He hastily answers questions before they are completed. Answer written questions before reading to the end.

(8) You have difficulty waiting your turn: in conversations, queues, restaurants.

(9) Often interrupt others in your activities and/or conversations.

It is necessary that the person has 5 or more symptoms to have a greater possibility of the diagnosis of Hyperactive/Impulsive ADHD.

Combined Type

It is necessary that the person has 5 or more symptoms of each of the above 2 groups for greater possibility of diagnosis of Combined Type ADHD.

IMPORTANT! In the diagnosis of **ADHD,** in addition to the above symptoms, the other criteria should also be observed:

A. Symptoms   (seen above).

B. Some of these symptoms should be present before 12 years of age.

C. There are problems caused by the above symptoms in at least 2 different contexts (work, in social life, college, marital and/or family relationship).

D. There are obvious problems in professional, social, family and/or affective life due to symptoms.

E. If there is another problem (such as depression, mental deficiency, psychosis, etc.), symptoms cannot be attributed exclusively to it.

ADHD — Screening Quiz for Adults

Developed in the early 1990s by Larry Jasper and Ivan Goldberg, ADHD — Screening Quiz for Adults is a screening assessment to verify the existence of **ADHD** in adults.

How to Use

The 24 items proposed below should be in harmony with how the appraised person behaved and felt for most of their adult life. If it has been generally one way but has recently changed, your answers should follow the reflection: "How Has This Person Been Generally?" Then, for each question presented, consider 1 of the 6 answers below that best matches the person evaluated.

1. **Never = 0 Points**
2. **Just A Little = 1 Point**
3. **Reasonably = 2 Points**
4. **Moderately = 3 Points**
5. **Most of the time = 4 Points**
6. **Very = 5 Points**

1. At home, at work or at school, I feel my mind moving away from uninteresting or difficult tasks.

( ) Never
( ) Just a little
( ) Reasonably
( ) Moderately
( ) Most of the time
( ) Very

2. I find it difficult to read written texts unless it's about something very interesting and/or very easy to read.

( ) Never
( ) Just a little
( ) Reasonably
( ) Moderately
( ) Most of the time
( ) Very

3. Especially in groups, I find it difficult to stay focused (a) on what is being said in the conversations.

( ) Never
( ) Just a little
( ) Reasonably
( ) Moderately
( ) Most of the time
( ) Very

4. I have an cranky temper and i'm usually "short wick."

( ) Never
( ) Just a little
( ) Reasonably
( ) Moderately
( ) Most of the time
( ) Very

5. I get angry easily and i get bored for little things.

( ) Never
( ) Just a little
( ) Reasonably
( ) Moderately

( ) Most of the time
( ) Very

6. Often, I say things without thinking, and then I regret saying them.

( ) Never
( ) Just a little
( ) Reasonably
( ) Moderately
( ) Most of the time
( ) Very

7. I generally make hasty decisions without assessing enough about its possible consequences.

( ) Never
( ) Just a little
( ) Reasonably
( ) Moderately
( ) Most of the time
( ) Very

8. I have problems in interpersonal relationships due to my tendency to speak first and think afterwards.

( ) Never
( ) Just a little
( ) Reasonably
( ) Moderately
( ) Most of the time
( ) Very

9. My mood oscillates from one end to the other, between ups and downs.

( ) Never
( ) Just a little
( ) Reasonably
( ) Moderately
( ) Most of the time
( ) Very

10. I have difficulty planning on what order should I follow to perform the tasks or activities.

( ) Never
( ) Just a little
( ) Reasonably
( ) Moderately
( ) Most of the time
( ) Very

11. I get bored (a) with ease.

( ) Never
( ) Just a little
( ) Reasonably
( ) Moderately
( ) Most of the time
( ) Very

12. I have low tolerance for negative reviews, and I am easily upset about it.

( ) Never
( ) Just a little
( ) Reasonably

( ) Moderately
( ) Most of the time
( ) Very

13. I'm almost always moving. I'm very agitated.

( ) Never
( ) Just a little
( ) Reasonably
( ) Moderately
( ) Most of the time
( ) Very

14. I feel more comfortable when I'm moving, than when I'm standing.

( ) Never
( ) Just a little
( ) Reasonably
( ) Moderately
( ) Most of the time
( ) Very

15. In conversations, I begin to answer the questions even before people formulate it entirely.

( ) Never
( ) Just a little
( ) Reasonably
( ) Moderately
( ) Most of the time
( ) Very

16. I usually work on more than one project at the same time, and normally, I end up not completing many of them.

( ) Never
( ) Just a little
( ) Reasonably
( ) Moderately
( ) Most of the time
( ) Very

17. There are always many internal ideas, thoughts and dialogues in my head, as a kind of "chatter".

( ) Never
( ) Just a little
( ) Reasonably
( ) Moderately
( ) Most of the time
( ) Very

18. Even when I'm sitting (a) silently, I usually keep moving my hands or feet.

( ) Never
( ) Just a little
( ) Reasonably
( ) Moderately
( ) Most of the time
( ) Very

19. In group activities, it is very difficult to have to wait my turn.

( ) Never

( ) Just a little
( ) Reasonably
( ) Moderately
( ) Most of the time
( ) Very

20. My mind is always so confused that it seems difficult to achieve a good mental functioning.

( ) Never
( ) Just a little
( ) Reasonably
( ) Moderately
( ) Most of the time
( ) Very

21. I think of several things simultaneously, and my thoughts seem to move as if my mind were an arcade machine.

( ) Never
( ) Just a little
( ) Reasonably
( ) Moderately
( ) Most of the time
( ) Very

22. My brain looks like a television set with all channels connected at the same time.

( ) Never
( ) Just a little
( ) Reasonably
( ) Moderately
( ) Most of the time
( ) Very

23. When I'm daydreaming it's even hard to stop "daydreaming."

( ) Never
( ) Just a little
( ) Reasonably
( ) Moderately
( ) Most of the time
( ) Very

24. I am distressed by the disorganized way of functioning my brain.

( ) Never
( ) Just a little
( ) Reasonably
( ) Moderately
( ) Most of the time
( ) Very

How to Evaluate

From 0 to 24 points — Probably has no **ADHD**

From 25 to 34 points — Has only a few symptoms of **ADHD**

From 35 to 49 points — The evaluated person probably has **ADHD** with average current severity.

From 50 to 69 points — The evaluated person probably has **ADHD** with moderate current severity.

Above 70 points — The evaluated person has **ADHD**

NOTE*: it should be taken into account even that, high scores in this exam can result from episodes of anxiety, depression or mania. These conditions should be discarded before a diagnosis of **ADHD** in adults can be confirmed.

Conners Evaluation Scales
–Versions for Parents and Teachers –

Among the most commonly used instruments today to verify the diagnostic characteristics of Attention Deficit Hyperactivity Disorder **(ADHD)** highlighted by conners rating scales, Conners Evaluation Scales — Versions for Parents and Teachers. Prepared in 1969 by the then American psychologist, Carmen Keith Conners, the scale was slightly adapted to other countries, and with its wide diffusion became one of the best evaluated tools to verify the presence of **ADHD** symptoms. However, despite all its efficacy recognized worldwide, because it presents a structure similar to that of a semi-structured interview, its application alone, cannot ratify the diagnosis of **ADHD.**

Conners Scale for Teachers - Reduced Version

Below are the most frequent problems that affect children during their developmental process. And while many of these characteristics are appropriate for normal behaviors, it should be carefully examined whether these manifestations have high levels of intensity, frequency and / or duration. Thus, the questions below should be answered considering the child's behavior during the last month. Therefore, it is recommended that, for each item, ask yourself, "How often has this happened in the last month?" Then, for each of the 28 propositions presented, mark 1 of the 4 answers below that best corresponds to the person evaluated.

1. **Never = 0 Points**
2. **A Little = 1 Point**
3. **Often = 2 Points**
4. **Very Often = 3 Points**

1. Inattentive (a). Easily get distracted

( ) Never
( ) A Little
( ) Often
( ) Very Often

2. Challenging behavior with adults

( ) Never
( ) A Little
( ) Often
( ) Very Often

3. Restless (a). It seems to have "carpenter animals" (stir so the body without leaving place)

( ) Never
( ) A Little
( ) Often
( ) Very Often

4. Forget things he (a) had already learned

( ) Never
( ) A Little
( ) Often
( ) Very Often

5. Disturbs other children

( ) Never
( ) A Little
( ) Often
( ) Very Often

6. Challenges the adult and does not collaborate with the requests made to him

( ) Never
( ) A Little
( ) Often
( ) Very Often

7. Move a lot as it is always "connected (a) to an engine"

( ) Never
( ) A Little
( ) Often
( ) Very Often

8. Spells poorly

( ) Never
( ) A Little
( ) Often
( ) Very Often

9. Can't stay quiet (a) for long

( ) Never
( ) A Little
( ) Often
( ) Very Often

10. Vengeful (a) or evil (a)

( ) Never
( ) A Little
( ) Often
( ) Very Often

11. You get up from the place in the classroom or in other situations where you should sit (a)

( ) Never
( ) A Little
( ) Often
( ) Very Often

12. Move your feet and/or hands and are restless (a) in your place

( ) Never
( ) A Little
( ) Often
( ) Very Often

13. Read capacity below expected

( ) Never
( ) A Little

( ) Often
( ) Very Often

14. Have a short time of attention

( ) Never
( ) A Little
( ) Often
( ) Very Often

15. Usually argue or challenge adults

( ) Never
( ) A Little
( ) Often
( ) Very Often

16. Directs attention only to matters that interest you

( ) Never
( ) A Little
( ) Often
( ) Very Often

17. Have difficulty waiting your turn

( ) Never
( ) A Little
( ) Often
( ) Very Often

18. Demonstrates disinterest in schoolwork

( ) Never
( ) A Little

( ) Often
( ) Very Often

19. Distracted (a) or presenting short attention time

( ) Never
( ) A Little
( ) Often
( ) Very Often

20. Has an explosive and unpredictable temperament

( ) Never
( ) A Little
( ) Often
( ) Very Often

21. Runs around space or over-galga in situations where such behaviors are inappropriate

( ) Never
( ) A Little
( ) Often
( ) Very Often

22. Poor in arithmetic

( ) Never
( ) A Little
( ) Often
( ) Very Often

23. Interrupt and/or intrude in the games or conversations of other

( ) Never
( ) A Little
( ) Often
( ) Very Often

24. Have difficulty engaging in games or leisure activities, in a quiet way

( ) Never
( ) A Little
( ) Often
( ) Very Often

25. Generally, it does not complete the things that begins

( ) Never
( ) A Little
( ) Often
( ) Very Often

26. It does not usually follow the instructions given to it and does not complete school activities (not due to opposition behaviors, nor because of a lack of understanding of what has been asked of)

( ) Never
( ) A Little
( ) Often
( ) Very Often

27. Excitable and impulsive (a)

( ) Never

( ) A Little
( ) Often
( ) Very Often

28. Restless (a). He's always getting up from the chair and moving around the room space.

( ) Never
( ) A Little
( ) Often
( ) Very Often

Conners Scale for Parents - Reduced Version

The following will be presented the most frequent problems affecting children during their development process. And, although many Dess the characteristics are appropriate to normal behaviors, it should be carefully analyzed if these manifestations present high values in intensity, frequency and/or duration levels. Thus, the questions below should be answered considering the behavior of the child during the last month. Therefore, it is recommended that, for each item, ask yourself, "How often has this occurred in the last month?" Then, for each of the 27 propositions presented, Marquand 1 of the 4 answers below that best corresponds to the evaluated person.

1. **Never = 0 Points**
2. **A Little = 1 Point**
3. **Often = 2 Points**
4. **Very Often = 3 Points**

1. Inattentive. Easily get distracted.

( ) Never
( ) A Little
( ) Often
( ) Very Often

2. Furious. It gets angry with ease and is resentful.

( ) Never

( ) A Little
( ) Often
( ) Very Often

3.Difficulty in doing or finishing homework

( ) Never
( ) A Little
( ) Often
( ) Very Often

4.You are always moving or acting as "having batteries charged" or as if "connected to an engine"

( ) Never
( ) A Little
( ) Often
( ) Very Often

5.Short attention time

( ) Never
( ) A Little
( ) Often
( ) Very Often

6.Discusses and/or argues with adults in an inappropriate manner

( ) Never
( ) A Little
( ) Often
( ) Very Often

7.Stir your feet and hands a lot and move even if you sit in place

( ) Never
( ) A Little
( ) Often
( ) Very Often

8.Generally, you can't and/or have difficulty completing your activities

( ) Never
( ) A Little
( ) Often
( ) Very Often

9.   Difficult to control in shopping centers or public places

( ) Never
( ) A Little
( ) Often
( ) Very Often

10.Messy and/or disorganized at home and/or school

( ) Never
( ) A Little
( ) Often
( ) Very Often

11. Irascible. Loses control with ease

( ) Never
( ) A Little

( ) Often
( ) Very Often

12. Need to be charged or accompanied to perform your tasks

( ) Never
( ) A Little
( ) Often
( ) Very Often

13. Only pay attention to things that interest you

( ) Never
( ) A Little
( ) Often
( ) Very Often

14. Runs around space or over-galga in situations where such behaviors are inappropriate

( ) Never
( ) A Little
( ) Often
( ) Very Often

15. Distracted (a) and/or with a short attention time

( ) Never
( ) A Little
( ) Often
( ) Very Often

16. Irritable

( ) Never
( ) A Little
( ) Often
( ) Very Often

17.Avoids, expresses reluctance or has difficulty in undertaking tasks that require continued mental effort (such as school or homework)

( ) Never
( ) A Little
( ) Often
( ) Very Often

18.Restless(a) it seems that "has carpenter sbugs" (stirs the body without leaving place)

( ) Never
( ) A Little
( ) Often
( ) Very Often

19.Get distracted when they're giving you instructions to do something

( ) Never
( ) A Little
( ) Often
( ) Very Often

20.Challenges the adult or refuses to satisfy the requests made to him

( ) Never
( ) A Little
( ) Often
( ) Very Often

21. Demonstrates concentration problems during classes

( ) Never
( ) A Little
( ) Often
( ) Very Often

22. Have difficulty staying in a queue or waiting for your turn in a game or group work

( ) Never
( ) A Little
( ) Often
( ) Very Often

23. Get up in the room or in places where you should sit

( ) Never
( ) A Little
( ) Often
( ) Very Often

24. Deliberately does things to annoy others

( ) Never
( ) A Little
( ) Often
( ) Very Often

25.Does not follow instructions and normally, does not terminate work, tasks and obligations in place (it is not difficult to understand instructions or refusal)

( ) Never
( ) A Little
( ) Often
( ) Very Often

26.Have difficulty playing or working quietly

( ) Never
( ) A Little
( ) Often
( ) Very Often

27.Get frustrated when you can't do anything

( ) Never
( ) A Little
( ) Often
( ) Very Often

Conners Scale for Parents and Teachers
Version adapted and validated for use in Brazil

Adapted and validated in Brazil by Barbosa in 1995, the integrated version of the Conners scale for parents and teachers consists of four factors distributed among 81 propositions, which are characterized by the resulting profile of children and/or adolescents with **ADHD.** Thus, while some scales investigate only the presence of current symptomatic manifestations, the Conners Evaluation Scales also allow, to analyze systematically, each of the symptoms contemplated by **DSM,** dating back to childhood and adolescence.

1. **Never = 0 Points**
2. **Sometimes = 1 Point**
3. **Often = 2 Points**
4. **Always = 3 Points**

Parent version - Cutoff point equal to 58

1. Usual behavior at home

Wakes up at night

( ) Never
( ) Sometimes
( ) Often
( ) Always

You're afraid in the face of new situations

( ) Never
( ) Sometimes
( ) Often
( ) Always

You're afraid of people

( ) Never
( ) Sometimes
( ) Often
( ) Always

You're afraid you're alone

( ) Never
( ) Sometimes
( ) Often
( ) Always

He cares about diseases and deaths

( ) Never
( ) Sometimes
( ) Often
( ) Always

It is tense and rigid

( ) Never
( ) Sometimes
( ) Often
( ) Always

Presents muscle spasms

( ) Never
( ) Sometimes
( ) Often
( ) Always

It presents tremors

( ) Never
( ) Sometimes
( ) Often
( ) Always

You feel headaches

( ) Never
( ) Sometimes
( ) Often
( ) Always

You feel stomach pains

( ) Never
( ) Sometimes
( ) Often
( ) Always

There's vomiting

( ) Never
( ) Sometimes
( ) Often
( ) Always

Complains of illnesses and pains

( ) Never

( ) Sometimes
( ) Often
( ) Always

Let yourself be carried away by other children

( ) Never
( ) Sometimes
( ) Often
( ) Always

Challenges and intimidates others

( ) Never
( ) Sometimes
( ) Often
( ) Always

He is brave (arrogant) and disrespects his superiors (insolent)

( ) Never
( ) Sometimes
( ) Often
( ) Always

It is brazen with adults

( ) Never
( ) Sometimes
( ) Often
( ) Always

He's shy in front of his friends

( ) Never
( ) Sometimes

( ) Often
( ) Always

Fear not to please your friends

( ) Never
( ) Sometimes
( ) Often
( ) Always

Have friends

( ) Never
( ) Sometimes
( ) Often
( ) Always

It's malicious with your brothers

( ) Never
( ) Sometimes
( ) Often
( ) Always

Fight constantly

( ) Never
( ) Sometimes
( ) Often
( ) Always

Criticizes many other children

( ) Never
( ) Sometimes
( ) Often

( ) Always

Learn in school

( ) Never
( ) Sometimes
( ) Often
( ) Always

Likes to go to school

( ) Never
( ) Sometimes
( ) Often
( ) Always

You're afraid to go to school

( ) Never
( ) Sometimes
( ) Often
( ) Always

Disobeys school standards

( ) Never
( ) Sometimes
( ) Often
( ) Always

Mind, blaming others for their mistakes

( ) Never
( ) Sometimes
( ) Often
( ) Always

Steals from your parents

( ) Never
( ) Sometimes
( ) Often
( ) Always

Performs thefts at school

( ) Never
( ) Sometimes
( ) Often
( ) Always

Steals in shops, tents and elsewhere

( ) Never
( ) Sometimes
( ) Often
( ) Always

You have problems with the police.

( ) Never
( ) Sometimes
( ) Often
( ) Always

You want to do everything well done (perfectionist)

( ) Never
( ) Sometimes
( ) Often
( ) Always

You always need to do things the same way

( ) Never
( ) Sometimes
( ) Often
( ) Always

It has great goals (dreams loudly)

( ) Never
( ) Sometimes
( ) Often
( ) Always

Easily get distracted

( ) Never
( ) Sometimes
( ) Often
( ) Always

It is nervous and restless

( ) Never
( ) Sometimes
( ) Often
( ) Always

Can't be quiet

( ) Never
( ) Sometimes
( ) Often
( ) Always

Rises everywhere

( ) Never

( ) Sometimes
( ) Often
( ) Always

Wakes up too early

( ) Never
( ) Sometimes
( ) Often
( ) Always

Don't be quiet during meals

( ) Never
( ) Sometimes
( ) Often
( ) Always

If you start doing something repetitive, you have difficulty stopping

( ) Never
( ) Sometimes
( ) Often
( ) Always

Their attitudes appear to be driven by an engine

( ) Never
( ) Sometimes
( ) Often
( ) Always

Teacher version - Cutoff point equal to 62

2. Classroom behavior

It's constantly moving

( ) Never
( ) Sometimes
( ) Often
( ) Always

Emits sounds, noises

( ) Never
( ) Sometimes
( ) Often
( ) Always

He likes that your orders will be slightly fulfilled

( ) Never
( ) Sometimes
( ) Often
( ) Always

Has compromised motor coordination

( ) Never
( ) Sometimes
( ) Often
( ) Always

Restless, superactive

( ) Never
( ) Sometimes
( ) Often
( ) Always

Excitable, impulsive

( ) Never
( ) Sometimes
( ) Often
( ) Always

Inattentive and easily distracted

( ) Never
( ) Sometimes
( ) Often
( ) Always

Normally, it does not end what begins

( ) Never
( ) Sometimes
( ) Often
( ) Always

Overly sensitive

( ) Never
( ) Sometimes
( ) Often
( ) Always

Extremely serious and/or sad

( ) Never
( ) Sometimes
( ) Often
( ) Always

Dream awakes

( ) Never
( ) Sometimes
( ) Often
( ) Always

Grumpy, grumpy

( ) Never
( ) Sometimes
( ) Often
( ) Always

Cry with ease

( ) Never
( ) Sometimes
( ) Often
( ) Always

Disturbs other children

( ) Never
( ) Sometimes
( ) Often
( ) Always

Causes confusion

( ) Never
( ) Sometimes
( ) Often
( ) Always

Mood oscillates dramatically and quickly

( ) Never

( ) Sometimes
( ) Often
( ) Always

Cunning, he likes to play the smart guy

( ) Never
( ) Sometimes
( ) Often
( ) Always

Destructive

( ) Never
( ) Sometimes
( ) Often
( ) Always

Iridescent

( ) Never
( ) Sometimes
( ) Often
( ) Always

Mind

( ) Never
( ) Sometimes
( ) Often
( ) Always

Bursts of anger, unpredictable, explosive behavior

( ) Never
( ) Sometimes

( ) Often
( ) Always

3. Group Participation

Isolates from other children

( ) Never
( ) Sometimes
( ) Often
( ) Always

It doesn't seem to be accepted by the group

( ) Never
( ) Sometimes
( ) Often
( ) Always

It seems to get carried away easily

( ) Never
( ) Sometimes
( ) Often
( ) Always

Does not demonstrate "sportsmanship"

( ) Never
( ) Sometimes
( ) Often
( ) Always

You don't seem to have leadership skills

( ) Never

( ) Sometimes
( ) Often
( ) Always

It doesn't relate well to the opposite sex

( ) Never
( ) Sometimes
( ) Often
( ) Always

It doesn't relate well to same-sex children

( ) Never
( ) Sometimes
( ) Often
( ) Always

It causes other children or interferes with their activities deliberately

( ) Never
( ) Sometimes
( ) Often
( ) Always

4. Attitude towards authorities

Submissive

( ) Never
( ) Sometimes
( ) Often
( ) Always

Challenging

( ) Never
( ) Sometimes
( ) Often
( ) Always

Sassy

( ) Never
( ) Sometimes
( ) Often
( ) Always

Shy

( ) Never
( ) Sometimes
( ) Often
( ) Always

Scared

( ) Never
( ) Sometimes
( ) Often
( ) Always

Excessive attention requirement. Mainly, from the teacher

( ) Never
( ) Sometimes
( ) Often
( ) Always

Stubborn

( ) Never

( ) Sometimes
( ) Often
( ) Always

Overly eager to please

( ) Never
( ) Sometimes
( ) Often
( ) Always

Non-cooperation

( ) Never
( ) Sometimes
( ) Often
( ) Always

Lack of classes often

( ) Never
( ) Sometimes
( ) Often
( ) Always

Structured Adults ADHD Self-Test (SAAST)

Developed by Dr. Greg Mulhauser, Structured Self-testing for adults with **ADHD** is a screening assessment that serves only as an indicative resource for the diagnosis of **ADHD** in adults. Formed by 22 questions that differ between two distinct components of the diagnosis of **ADHD** (inattention along with hyperactivity/impulsivity) this tool is also sensitive to factors that normally prevent the diagnosis of **ADHD.**

How to Use

According to the values presented for the 4 response options, the 22 sentences proposed below should correspond to the way the person evaluated felt and behaved during most of their adult life.

1.   **No, no way = 0 Points**
2.   **Yes, a little = 1 Point**
3.   **Yes, moderately = 2 Points**
4.   **Yes, very = 3 Points**

1. I found that I made mistakes at work, at school, or in other activities because I have difficulty paying attention to the details.

( ) No, no way

( ) Yes, a little

( ) Yes, moderately

( ) Yes, very

2. I tend to mess with my hands, feet, or squirm, often, in places that should remain quiet.

( ) No, no way

( ) Yes, a little

( ) Yes, moderately

( ) Yes, very

3. I often get distracted and lose myself in what's being said in conversations.

( ) No, no way

( ) Yes, a little

( ) Yes, moderately

( ) Yes, very

4. I prefer to run or climb things, even when I know it doesn't fit the situation.

( ) No, no way

( ) Yes, a little

( ) Yes, moderately

( ) Yes, very

5. I find it difficult to organize my tasks and/or activities.

( ) No, no way

( ) Yes, a little

( ) Yes, moderately

( ) Yes, very

6. I'm often "on the go."

( ) No, no way

( ) Yes, a little

( ) Yes, moderately

( ) Yes, very

7. I usually lose things I need to use not school or not work.

( ) No, no way

( ) Yes, a little

( ) Yes, moderately

( ) Yes, very

8. I can't help but answer before someone's even done asking me a question.

( ) No, no way

( ) Yes, a little

( ) Yes, moderately

( ) Yes, very

9. I am forgotten during my daily activities.

( ) No, no way

( ) Yes, a little

( ) Yes, moderately

( ) Yes, very

10. I find it difficult to keep my attention on what I'm doing, whether it's working or playing.

( ) No, no way

( ) Yes, a little

( ) Yes, moderately

( ) Yes, very

11. I find it hard to sit, even when I know I need to wait for something.

( ) No, no way

( ) Yes, a little

( ) Yes, moderately

( ) Yes, very

12. I find it difficult to follow instructions or complete tasks or duties, even understanding that is what is expected of me.

( ) No, no way

( ) Yes, a little

( ) Yes, moderately

( ) Yes, very

13. I find it difficult to engage in playful activities athleisure u that are silent.

( ) No, no way

( ) Yes, a little

( ) Yes, moderately

( ) Yes, very

14. I don't like having to do something that requires sustained mental effort.

( ) No, no way

( ) Yes, a little

( ) Yes, moderately

( ) Yes, very

15. I usually talk excessively.

( ) No, no way

( ) Yes, a little

( ) Yes, moderately

( ) Yes, very

16. I'm easily distracted.

( ) No, no way

( ) Yes, a little

( ) Yes, moderately

( ) Yes, very

17. I have trouble waiting my turn.

( ) No, no way

( ) Yes, a little

( ) Yes, moderately

( ) Yes, very

18. I often interrupt others.

( ) No, no way

( ) Yes, a little

( ) Yes, moderately

( ) Yes, very

19. Even before the age of 7, some of the previous questions (1-18) would still have been marked "Yes, moderately" or "Yes, too".

( ) No

( ) Yes

20. I have problems related to some of the above situations in more than one context. That is, I have manifestations of these problems not only at home, nor only at work.

( ) No

( ) Yes

21. The presence of these problems usually triggers some harm and social, academic, professional and/or my interpersonal relationships.

( ) No, no way

( ) Yes, a little

( ) Yes, moderately

( ) Yes, very

22. I have been diagnosed before with another **Disorder which could also justify** the types **of experiences proposed above. Or I believe you might be going through such a mess. This may include Invasive Developmental Disorder, Mood Disorder, Anxiety Disorder, Dissociative Disorder, Personality Disorder, Schizophrenia or other Psychotic Disorder.**

( ) No

( ) Yes

How to Evaluate

Score for questions 1-18:
0 — No, no way
1 — Yes, a little
2 — Yes, moderately
3 — Yes, very

This produces a total maximum score of 54. Question 21 is scored on the same scale; however, it is used to judge whether an **ADHD** diagnosis should be excluded. Therefore, it should not be included in the final total of the points. Questions 19, 20 and 22 with the possibility of answers only to YES / NO scored as a binary choice and are used again to rule out the diagnosis of **ADHD**. For example, question 19 about the presence of symptoms before age 7.

Additional Information

Scores above 24, along with the absence of mitigating factors (other medical conditions) are generally consistent for the presence of **ADHD.** Therefore, if the evaluated person obtained more than 24 points in this test it is recommended that him seek an expert to perform a more detailed and accurate evaluation.

Initial Questionnaire for Parents and Teachers

Composed of 120 sentences, the integrated version of the Initial Questionnaire for Parents (QIPAIS) and the Initial Questionnaire for Teachers (QIPROF) was developed by joining the characteristics present in 4 different tools used in the diagnosis of **ADHD**: **(1)** DSM, **(2)** Child Behavior Checklist (CBCL), **(3)** and Scala de Conners, **(4)** SNAP-IV.

How to Use

Following will be related to the descriptive terms of behavior of your student (a) or child(a). Read, carefully, each item, and according to the 5 abbreviated response options below, check the one that best matches the evaluated person.

1. **Never / Not A Little = (NL)**
2. **Sometimes / Rarely = (SR)**
3. **Oftentimes / Frequently = (OF)**
4. **Always = (A)**
5. **Don't Know Inform= (DKI)**

1. Failure to pay attention to detail or make mistakes for lack of care in schoolwork and tasks

(N L)

(S R)

(O F)

(A)

(D K I)

2. Difficulty finishing what begins

(N L)

(S R)

(O F)

(A)

(D K I)

3. It is disorganized in your class lessons, tasks or activities

(N L)

(S R)

(O F)

(A)

(D K I)

4. Forget daily activities (tasks, errands, obligations)

(N L)

(S R)

(O F)

(A)

(D K I)

5. Doesn't seem to hear when they talk to him

(N L)

(S R)

(O F)

(A)

(D K I)

6. Unable to pay attention to the same thing for a long time

(N L)

(S R)

(O F)

(A)

(D K I)

7. Have difficulties to follow instructions, terminate homework, tasks, or obligations

(N L)

(S R)

(O F)

(A)

(D K I)

8. Easily distracted by noises or other stimuli in class

(N L)

(S R)

(O F)

(A)

(D K I)

9. Avoids, dislikes or refutes in participating in tasks and games that require mental effort

(N L)

(S R)

(O F)

(A)

(D K I)

10. Loses things (toys, books, pencils, notebooks, jackets, slippers)

(N L)

(S R)

(O F)

(A)

(D K I)

11. Has difficulty staying tuned during explanations, to respond to requests or execute orders

(N L)

(S R)

(O F)

(A)

(D K I)

12. Have difficulty keeping an eye on tasks or games

(N L)

(S R)

(O F)

(A)

(D K I)

13. Lives dreaming, in the "world of the moon"

(N L)

(S R)

(O F)

(A)

(D K I)

14. Difficulty in paying attention to an activity or conversation

(N L)

(S R)

(O F)

(A)

(D K I)

15. Quickly forget what has just been said

(N L)

(S R)

(O F)

(A)

(D K I)

16. School activities are usually delayed

(N L)

(S R)

(O F)

(A)

(D K I)

17. Difficulty in fulfilling orders

(N L)

(S R)

(O F)

(A)

(D K I)

18. Difficulty following instructions

(N L)

(S R)

(O F)

(A)

(D K I)

19. Difficulty to wait the turn

(N L)

(S R)

(O F)

(A)

(D K I)

20. Age recklessly (risks)

(N L)

(S R)

(O F)

(A)

(D K I)

21. Do tasks quickly to feel livre.

(N L)

(S R)

(O F)

(A)

(D K I)

22. Answer before hearing any question

(N L)

(S R)

(O F)

(A)

(D K I)

23. It always appears to be "at full steam" or "connected in an engine"

(N L)

(S R)

(O F)

(A)

(D K I)

24. Acts without thinking (it's impulsive)

(N L)

(S R)

(O F)

(A)

(D K I)

25. Interrupt or intrude in conversations, pranks

(N L)

(S R)

(O F)

(A)

(D K I)

26. Too much speech (hinders class)

(N L)

(S R)

(O F)

(A)

(D K I)

27. Have difficulty to stay sitting. If it stirs and/or rises from the chairs

(N L)

(S R)

(O F)

(A)

(D K I)

28. Have difficulty playing or silently participating in leisure activities

(N L)

(S R)

(O F)

(A)

(D K I)

29. Too much conversation (disrupts the environment or class)

(N L)

(S R)

(O F)

(A)

(D K I)

30. Runs or climbs through the walls in inappropriate situations

(N L)

(S R)

(O F)

(A)

(D K I)

31. It is impatient and restless

(N L)

(S R)

(O F)

(A)

(D K I)

32. Requires your requests to be met immediately

(N L)

(S R)

(O F)

(A)

(D K I)

33. Shakes hands and feet and shakes in chair/wallet

(N L)

(S R)

(O F)

(A)

(D K I)

34. Breaks or destroys school material or other objects

(N L)

(S R)

(O F)

(A)

(D K I)

35. Suffers Accidents Easily

(N L)

(S R)

(O F)

(A)

(D K I)

36. Speaks with difficulty

(N L)

(S R)

(O F)

(A)

(D K I)

37. Difficulty in drafting texts (summarizing, lack of content or coherence)

(N L)

(S R)

(O F)

(A)

(D K I)

38. Slow reading, silachia, faltering, non-automated

(N L)

(S R)

(O F)

(A)

(D K I)

39. Difficulty in interpreting texts read

(N L)

(S R)

(O F)

(A)

(DKI)

40. Difficulty in interpreting written texts

(NL)

(SR)

(OF)

(A)

(DKI)

41. Presents difficulties in writing: exchanges, substitutions, mirroring or agglutination

(NL)

(SR)

(OF)

(A)

(DKI)

42. Presents sloppy calligraphy

(NL)

(SR)

(OF)

(A)

(DKI)

43. Presents inadequate accentuation and scores

(N L)

(S R)

(O F)

(A)

(D K I)

44. Logical reasoning is slow

(N L)

(S R)

(O F)

(A)

(D K I)

45. Failure to solve mathematical problems

(N L)

(S R)

(O F)

(A)

(D K I)

46. Performs mathematical operations with difficulty (according to series)

(N L)

(S R)

(O F)

(A)

(D K I)

47. Yields below expected at school

(N L)

(S R)

(O F)

(A)

(D K I)

48. Have difficulty expressing your thoughts orally

(N L)

(S R)

(O F)

(A)

(D K I)

49. Avoids tasks that require constant mental effort

(N L)

(S R)

(O F)

(A)

(D K I)

50. Presents difficulty in fine motricity (drawings, lace, tie, button, use scissors)

(N L)

(S R)

(O F)

(A)

(D K I)

51. Presents difficulty in global motricity (balance, falls frequently)

(N L)

(S R)

(O F)

(A)

(D K I)

52. Avoids school tasks or work

(N L)

(S R)

(O F)

(A)

(D K I)

53. Avoids studying (lack of motivation to study and do tasks)

(N L)

(S R)

(O F)

(A)

(D K I)

54. Participates little in class and asks for help when necessary

(N L)

(S R)

(O F)

(A)

(D K I)

55. Studies little for evaluations

(N L)

(S R)

(O F)

(A)

(D K I)

56. Loses calm easily (short wick)

(N L)

(S R)

(O F)

(A)

(D K I)

57. Discusses with adults (cheeky, debauched, bold)

(N L)

(S R)

(O F)

(A)

(D K I)

58. It is bully or aggressive with other people

(N L)

(S R)

(O F)

(A)

(D K I)

59. Challenges or refuses to follow the rules or requests/requests such as brushing your teeth, bathing, doing chores

(N L)

(S R)

(O F)

(A)

(D K I)

60. Does purpose-based things that bother or interfere with the activities

(N L)

(S R)

(O F)

(A)

(D K I)

61. Blames others for their errors or misconduct

(N L)

(S R)

(O F)

(A)

(D K I)

62. Disturbs other children (irritates other children with antics, jerks or pokes)

(N L)

(S R)

(O F)

(A)

(D K I)

63. It is brave and/or resentful

(N L)

(S R)

(O F)

(A)

(D K I)

64. Hate guard or is vengeful

(N L)

(S R)

(O F)

(A)

(D K I)

65. Is a negativist, defiant, disobedient or hostile against

(N L)

(S R)

(O F)

(A)

(D K I)

66. Hurts other children

(N L)

(S R)

(O F)

(A)

(D K I)

67. Steal something (money, school supplies, toys)

(N L)

(S R)

(O F)

(A)

(D K I)

68. Easily frustrated if not met

(N L)

(S R)

(O F)

(A)

(D K I)

69. It's grumpy

(N L)

(S R)

(O F)

(A)

(D K I)

70. Destroys the property of the other people (vandalism)

(N L)

(S R)

(O F)

(A)

(D K I)

71. He is a liar (mind, fraud, glue, copies work, cheats)

(N L)

(S R)

(O F)

(A)

(D K I)

72. Violates the rules seriously - gauze class, flees, ignores class rules

(N L)

(S R)

(O F)

(A)

(D K I)

73. Cooperates little with teachers and/or colleagues

(N L)

(S R)

(O F)

(A)

(D K I)

74. Acts smartly (rascal), always wants to take advantage

(N L)

(S R)

(O F)

(A)

(D K I)

75. Is manipulator

(N L)

(S R)

(O F)

(A)

(D K I)

76. Presents access of fury / has explosive temperament

(N L)

(S R)

(O F)

(A)

(D K I)

77. It is rejected by colleagues or family members

(N L)

(S R)

(O F)

(A)

(D K I)

78. Difficulties in accepting limits

(N L)

(S R)

(O F)

(A)

(D K I)

79. Causes confusion in meetings, parties, parks or classroom

(N L)

(S R)

(O F)

(A)

(D K I)

80. It's sad, empty or unhappy

(N L)

(S R)

(O F)

(A)

(D K I)

81. Cries Easy

(N L)

(S R)

(O F)

(A)

(D K I)

82. Feels guilty or useless or incapable or finds it ugly

(N L)

(S R)

(O F)

(A)

(D K I)

83. Lack of interest or pleasure in activities (discouragement or tasteless for things or indisposition)

(N L)

(S R)

(O F)

(A)

(D K I)

84. Get tired

(N L)

(S R)

(O F)

(A)

(D K I)

85. Presents exaggerated lack or appetite

(N L)

(S R)

(O F)

(A)

(D K I)

86. Isolates or plays only

(N L)

(S R)

(O F)

(A)

(D K I)

87. Talks about dying or having ideas, plans or suicide attempt

(N L)

(S R)

(O F)

(A)

(D K I)

88. Persistent physical symptoms - headache, or abdominal or legs, diarrhea, vomiting, dizziness

(N L)

(S R)

(O F)

(A)

(D K I)

89. Have anxiety or excessive concern

(N L)

(S R)

(O F)

(A)

(D K I)

90. Presents low self-esteem most of the time

(N L)

(S R)

(O F)

(A)

(D K I)

91. Inconsequential in their acts (it does not care about the opinion of others)

(N L)

(S R)

(O F)

(A)

(D K I)

92. It is pessimistic, discouraged or hopeless

(NL)

(SR)

(OF)

(A)

(DKI)

93. Variable mood (sadness and/or irritability)

(NL)

(SR)

(OF)

(A)

(DKI)

94. Has fears or crises of panic

(NL)

(SR)

(OF)

(A)

(DKI)

95. It has compulsions (repetitive behaviors or acts to reduce anxiety or anguish: cleaning mania, checking if the door is open, repetition how to count numbers etc.)

(NL)

(SR)

(O F)

(A)

(D K I)

96. Has manias or rituals

(N L)

(S R)

(O F)

(A)

(D K I)

97. Speaks or makes intentional obscene gestures

(N L)

(S R)

(O F)

(A)

(D K I)

98. Makes strange noises (sniffle, strange sounds, profanity)

(N L)

(S R)

(O F)

(A)

(D K I)

99. It has some nerve tic (blinks, stirs with hands, shoulders,

arms, nail roi, sucks fingers)

(N L)

(S R)

(O F)

(A)

(D K I)

100. Worries about illness or death

(N L)

(S R)

(O F)

(A)

(D K I)

101. Presents euphoria, exaggerated or inappropriate joy

(N L)

(S R)

(O F)

(A)

(D K I)

102. Ideas of greatness, thinks "the best"

(N L)

(S R)

(O F)

(A)

(DKI)

103. Brave - faces situations inconsequentially

(NL)

(SR)

(OF)

(A)

(DKI)

104. Inappropriate sexual behavior (force sexual act, abuse, misconduct)

(NL)

(SR)

(OF)

(A)

(DKI)

105. Avoids looking into the eyes of others

(NL)

(SR)

(OF)

(A)

(DKI)

106. Presents abnormal movements (jumps, claps, shakes

hands, touches people)

(N L)

(S R)

(O F)

(A)

(D K I)

107. It's selfish

(N L)

(S R)

(O F)

(A)

(D K I)

108. Acts incorrectly: eliminates gases, spit, pushes others

(N L)

(S R)

(O F)

(A)

(D K I)

109. Difficulty memorizing

(N L)

(S R)

(O F)

(A)

(D K I)

110. Injures and harms animals (cruel)

(N L)

(S R)

(O F)

(A)

(D K I)

111. Starts fights or physical struggles

(N L)

(S R)

(O F)

(A)

(D K I)

112. Usually intimidates or threatens others

(N L)

(S R)

(O F)

(A)

(D K I)

113. Usually leaves urine or feces in clothes

(N L)

(S R)

(O F)

(A)

(D K I)

114. Constantly varies from behavior (sadness/euphoria/agitation)

(N L)

(S R)

(O F)

(A)

(D K I)

115. Concerns about the future (with things before it happens)

(N L)

(S R)

(O F)

(A)

(D K I)

116. It is undecided

(N L)

(S R)

(O F)

(A)

(D K I)

117. Concerns about past facts

(N L)

(S R)

(O F)

(A)

(D K I)

118. He's usually angry

(N L)

(S R)

(O F)

(A)

(D K I)

119. Presents obsessive, unpleasant, uncomfortable thoughts

(N L)

(S R)

(O F)

(A)

(D K I)

120. Presents sleep problems (insomnia, nightmares, sleepwalking, sleeping talk)

(N L)

(S R)

(O F)

(A)

(D K I)

Considerations

1. The difficulties presented above interfere and/or hinder his learning:

No ( )

Yes ( )

Do not know ( )

2. The difficulties presented above interfere and/or hinder his relationship with other children, teachers, school staff and/or family members:

No ( )

Yes ( )

Do not know ( )

Wender Utah Assessment Scale for ADHD

Consisting of 61 items and a subset with 25 questions associated with the diagnosis of **ADHD,** the Wender Utah Rating Scale (WURS), Wender Utah Evaluation Scale is a self-report instrument designed for retrospective dimensional evaluation of **ADHD** in childhood for adults and has been widely used in this context. According to the latest research it has also been found that the scale can be used appropriately to predict cases of dysthymia, oppositional defiant disorder, schoolwork problems, conduct disorder, and anxiety disorders in adults with ADHD. Based on the DSM criteria, the Wender Utah Rating Scale measures adult ADHD symptoms through seven categories:

1. Attention Difficulties;
2. Hyperactivity/Restlessness;
3. Temperament;
4. Affective Lability;
5. Emotional Hyper-Reactivity;
6. Disorganization;
7. Impulsivity;

How to Use

The 61 sentences should be answered by the adult evaluated, considering their behaviors during childhood (As a child, I was or had...). And from its conclusions, point out the value for response options that best represents the condition of the evaluated person.

1. **Not a little or too slightly = 0 Points**
2. **Smoothly = 1 Point**
3. **Moderately = 2 Points**
4. **Quite = 3 Points**
5. **Very = 4 Points**

As a child, I was (or had)

1.Active, agitated and was always on the move

2.I was afraid of many things

3.Concentration problems, easily distracted

4.Worry, anxiety

5.Nervous, restless

6.Unattentive, "dreamed awake"

7.Boiling point, "low or high" temperature

8.Sensitive shy

9.Explosive temperament, anger accesses

10.Difficulty with persistence to finish the things that began

11.Stubborn, obstinate

12.Sad, unhappy or depressed

13.Incauta and/or diabolical in the games

14.Didn't enjoy things, dissatisfied with life

15.Rebellious, disobedient and sassy with my parents

16.Low opinion about myself

17.Irritable

18.Extroverted and friendly in the company of persons

19.Sloppy, disorganized

20.High and low mood

21.Brava

22.Popular friends

23.Well organized, tidy

24.Acting impulsively, without thinking

25.Tendency to be immature

26. Feelings of guilt, of repentant

27.Lost control of myself

28.Tendency to be or act irrationally

29.Unpopular with other children, I didn't keep friends for long, I didn't relate well to other children

30. Uncoordinated, did not participate in sports

31.Fear of losing control

32.Had good motor coordination, was the first choice in games

33.Brazen (women only)

34.Run away from home

35.Engaged in fights

36.Teasing other children

37.Leader, bossy

38.Difficulty waking up

39.It was a follower, conducted too

40.Difficulty seeing things from someone else's point of view

41.Problems with authorities, school visits to the principal's office

42.Problems with the police

Medical problems as a child

43. Headaches
44. Stomach pains
45. Constipation prison
46. Diarrhea
47. Some food allergies
48. Other allergies
49. Enuresis

As a child at school I was (or had)

50. In general, an average student
51. In general, a poor student, slow learning
52. It took me a while to learn to read
53. Slow reader
54. Difficulty reversing the letters
55. Spelling problems
56. Problems with math and/or numbers
57. Bad calligraphy
58. Able to read very well, but never really liked to read
59. Did not reach the expected potential
60. Repeated low notes
61. Suspended or expelled

25 ADHD-Related Questions

3. Concentration problems, easily distracted
4. Concerns, anxiety
5. Nervous, restless

6. Inattentive, "dreamed awake"

7. Boiling point, "low or high" temperature

9. Explosive temperament, anger accesses

10. Difficulty with persistence to finish the things that began

11. Stubborn, stubborn

12. Sad, unhappy or depressed

15. Rebellious, disobedient and sassy with my parents

16. Low opinion on myself

17. Irritable

20. Mood changes, high and low in temperament

21. Brava

24. Acting impulsively, without thinking

25. Tendency to be immature

26. Feelings of guilt, of repentant

27. Losing control of myself

28. Tendency to be or act irrationally

29. Unpopular with other children, I did not keep friends for long, I did not relate well to other children

40. Difficulty in seeing things from someone else's point of view

41. Problems with authorities, school visits to the principal's office

As a child at school I was (or had)

51   In general, a poor student with slow learning

56. Problems with numbers, calculations and mathematics

59. Not reaching the expected potential

How to Evaluate

The sum of the 25 **ADHD-related** questions is used to calculate a summary **ADHD** score. Because the Wender Utah Evaluation Scale does not separately classify the **ADHD** (presentation specifiers) subtypes. The **ADHD** summary score cannot be integrated with other subtype scores.

WURS Subscore = _________ (sum of 25 **ADHD**-related questions)

A score below 50 indicates that **ADHD** symptoms are not consistent with a positive diagnosis for attention deficit.

A score greater than or equal to 50 indicates that **ADHD** symptoms are consistent with a positive diagnosis for attention deficit.

The summary score increases as the severity of **ADHD** responses increases. The summary score, therefore, is calculated by adding the answers to the 25 **ADHD**-related questions and using a cutoff of 46.

About The Writer

Marcus Deminco (Salvador-BA. Set, 28 1976). Brazilian writer and psychologist; Doctor Honoris Causa in Attention Deficit Disorder/Hyperactivity Disorder; Practitioner and Tutor of Neuro-linguistic programming (NLP); Portal of Psychologists Newsletter Subscriber. Wrote several texts, phrases and thoughts shared on numerous websites and social networks. Author of 'Why read Paulo Coelho?' Praised and shared by Paulo Coelho himself among his readers. Marcus Deminco is author of:

1) Me and My Friend ADD - Autobiography of a guy with Attention Deficit Disorder.

2) The Secret of Clarice Lispector

3) VERTYGO - The Suicide of Lukas (Portuguese Edition)

4) VERTYGO - The Suicide of Lukas (English Edition)

5) Neuro-Linguistic Programming: beginning by the beginning.

6) Messages to Post, Like and Share. Vol. 1

7) Messages to Post, Like and Share. Vol. 2

8) Messages to Post, Like and Share. Vol. 3

9) E-cards text collection. Vol. 1

10) E-cards text collection. Vol. 2

Awards and Tributes

1.1. Author of 'Estafeta Sem Rumo' – Cecilio Barros Barros Pessoa Awards of Anthology – Academy of Letters, Arts and Sciences of Arraial do Cabo - RJ.

1.2. Doctor Honoris Causa in ADHD by the Brazilian Association of Psychosomatic Medicine in recognition of the scientific contribution and social relevance of the book: Me & My Friend ADHD – Autobiography of a guy with Attention Deficit Disorder.

1.3. One of the winners of *Além da Terra, Além do Céu* prize of contemporary Brazilian poetry awarded by Chiado Editora.

Talk to Marcus Deminco

E-mail: marcusdeminco@gmail.com
Website: http://marcusdeminco.com/
Blog: http://marcusdeminco.blogspot.com.br/
Twitter: https://twitter.com/marcusdeminco
Facebook: https://www.facebook.com/marcus.deminco
Pinterest: https://www.pinterest.com/marcusdeminco/
Instagram: @marcusdeminco
Youtube: https://www.youtube.com/channel/UCRu8yfSoLewjuX6GO6o7Nmw
Tumblr: http://deminco.tumblr.com/
Flickr: https://www.flickr.com/photos/143729713@N06/with/28004881736/
GoodReads: https://www.goodreads.com/author/show/7792932.Marcus_Deminco/
Pensador: https://pensador.uol.com.br/autor/marcus_deminco/